50 Ways to
Feed Your Lover

"I have friends who begin with pasta,

and friends who begin with rice,

but whenever I fall in love,

I begin with potatoes."

—NORA EPHRON, *HEARTBURN*

50 Ways to Feed Your Lover

America's Top Chefs Share

Their Recipes and

Secrets for Romance

Janeen A. Sarlin and

Jennifer Rosenfeld Saltiel

WILLIAM MORROW AND COMPANY, INC.
New York

Spaghetti with Watercress and Garlic, and Roasted Sausages with Grapes, adapted from *Cucina Simpatica* by Johanne Killeen and George Germon, HarperCollins, 1991

Grilled Dover Sole with Golden Pepper Coulis and Parsley Essence, and Dark Chocolate Mousse, reprinted with permission from *Le Bec Fin Recipes* by Georges Perrier, Running Press, 1997

It is the policy of William Morrow and Company, Inc., and its imprints and affiliates, recognizing the importance of preserving what has been written, to print the books we publish on acid-free paper, and we exert our best efforts to that end.

Library of Congress Cataloging-in-Publication Data

Sarlin, Janeen.
    50 ways to feed your lover : America's top chefs share their recipes and secrets for romance / Janeen A. Sarlin and Jennifer Rosenfeld
    Saltiel. —1st ed.
        p.   cm.
    ISBN 0-688-16213-4
    1. Cookery.   2. Menus.   I. Saltiel, Jennifer Rosenfeld.
    II. Title.
    TX714.S284   2000
642'.4—dc21   99–33171
                                                   CIP

Printed in the United States of America

First Edition

1   2   3   4   5   6   7   8   9   10

BOOK DESIGN BY DONNA SINISGALLI

www.williammorrow.com

With love from Janeen to the men in my life

who have tasted with the same fork

and sipped from the same glass.

And with love from Jenny to my husband, Philip,

who has taught me everything about love, life, and good food.

Acknowledgments

They say that too many cooks spoil the broth, but here we celebrate fifty chefs for recounting their amorous tales and imparting the secret recipes of their sybaritic repertoire.

Both Janeen and Jenny want to thank Justin Schwartz, our editor, whose fleeting-glance interest became a real commitment. We offer baskets of chocolate chocolate–chip cookies to all those at William Morrow whose labors of love produced a book both romantic and practical. We send mounds of caviar to Paige Sarlin for her keen prose and the enthusiastic passion that worked wonders on the manuscript. If the road to gluttony leads straight to lust, then bravo to the special friends who lovingly devoured many test dinners chez Janeen. Jenny sends sweet dreams to her parents, Helaine and Karl Rosenfeld, for their unwavering love and support—both spiritually and financially—thanks her mother for listening to every word of this book and to her brother Billy for teaching her a different way to be . . . and a special hug to Rachel Fishman for her editorial insight.

Contents

MY HUSBAND, PHILIP, a sexy doctor with a knack in the kitchen, is usually in charge of dinner, romantic or otherwise. Each year for my birthday, I am treated to a meal filled with gourmet goodies such as butternut squash risotto, Dover sole baked in butter and lemon, and my favorite chocolate-chip cookies, all lovingly prepared from his library of cookbooks. The first time I saw all those books I was scoping out his apartment after our second official date. There were dozens of them stacked in rows. "Do you cook?" he had asked. "Oh, yes," I had lied. Delighted that he had found a culinary soul mate, he proceeded to show me his favorite recipes and even suggested that we make dinner together sometime. If Phil wanted spaghetti ragù, I said, he was in for a treat. A smarter woman would have bolted for the door; I stayed.

For months my lie went undetected thanks to a long list of excuses. I have to work late, the oven is broken, the dog ate the ingredients . . . I have a headache. Fortunately, the vast array of prepared foods available at gourmet take-outs bailed me out every time.

It wasn't until after we were engaged that my luck ran out. Phil wanted a home-cooked dinner for his birthday. Bribes of new stereos and cars were declined. I was stuck. So, on the eve of his birthday, I sifted through his cookbooks trying to piece together some semblance of a menu—one that would prove not only my undying love but also my culinary wizardry. When the big day arrived, I sweated for hours over my tiny stove, bouncing between stirring risotto and sautéing red snapper. I even whipped up an inadvertently fallen chocolate cake.

The risotto was crunchy, the fish had no taste, but Phil never said so. He just kept on eating, making approving grunts and gestures. When he finished the last bite, he told me it was the best meal anyone had ever cooked for him. That's when I knew he must be in love.

Despite my culinary breakthrough, I was back on the spaghetti sauce in no time. When Phil's next birthday rolled around, I happily made reservations at Felidia, an Italian restaurant in New York City. The evening went off without a hitch—as Phil said. Deliciously prepared entrées, flowing wine, and fresh flowers—a thoroughly enjoyable and relaxing experience. So delightful that I was inspired to try cooking another meal at home. Hoping to expand my repertoire, I quizzed the owner, Lidia Bastianich, who replied, "I can win any man's heart with a bowl of pasta!" It wasn't long before I was accosting chefs all over town—much to Phil's embarrassment —demanding to know their menus and their secrets of seductive cooking.

"I like to start with at least a hundred grams of caviar served in silver bowls," said Carole Peck up in Connecticut at The Good News Café. "Sometimes a hundred isn't even enough." At Mesa Grill chef Bobby Flay gave me more advice: Have all of the ingredients on hand before you begin cooking. You don't want to run out to the store an hour before your date arrives. Diane Forley at Verbena stressed the importance of a beautiful setting. "You can't just serve a dish and expect it to work on its own," she said. "It takes the lighting, the music, and the setting to achieve sensuality and romance."

One afternoon in my yoga class I found myself gabbing away with Janeen. When I discovered she was a chef, I knew it had to be a sign.

I decided to take up her offer of cooking lessons. As I cut, chopped, and peeled my way through the basics, I was no longer afraid to make mistakes. When I was ready to take the plunge, Janeen gave me ten simple secrets for seduction:

> Make a date.
> Plan the menu.
> Go food shopping and read the recipe twice.
> Clean the house.
> Set the stage: candles, linens, flowers, and music.
> Do the food preparations.

Relax, breathe, and take a bath.
Take another breath.
Get dressed.
Light the candles, put on the music, open the door, and let the
    seduction begin.

Feeding your lover isn't easy, but the rewards are great. So proceed with
confidence. The menus are right there, all you have to do is follow your
heart—and the directions.

—JRS

APHRODISIACS

Some foods don't require a lot of preparation to do wonders for your love life. The presentation alone will speak volumes. In fact, the mere mention of certain delicacies is enough. Around the world and over the centuries, caviar, champagne, chocolate, and oysters are foods that have acquired a reputation for producing results. All of the chefs whose recipes are in this book mentioned them—and fifty chefs can't be wrong.

Caviar: Aphrodite's Pearls

Aphrodite, the goddess of love, comes from the sea. It is no surprise, then, that caviar, the most regal of delicacies, is one of our chefs' favorite seductive foods. In most romances, timing, attention to detail, and the lavishing of thoughtful consideration reap the greatest harvest. So, too, with caviar. These black (sometimes gray or amber) pearls are expensive because of the number of years it takes for each fish to produce them and because of the care with which they must be treated.

The air of Russian mystery that surrounds caviar doesn't have to deter you from making educated choices when you lavish this extravagance on your prince or princess. The three most commonly available caviars come from sturgeon that swim in the Caspian Sea. There are many other types of caviar, including some American caviars, that are harvested from other species of fish, but the Russian morsels are considered the best.

Beluga caviar is the rarest and most coveted, for the sturgeon take twenty-five years to produce eggs. The eggs are large and vary in color from light gray to nearly black. For status, beluga is *the* caviar. Clearly you are willing to spare no expense. The creamy texture of beluga distinguishes it from other caviars. It has a rich flavor and is slightly salty, with hints of metal or mineral.

Osetra caviar is the next most prized, being produced after only twelve years. The roe has a dark golden hue when the fish are young and fades to pale amber as the sturgeons age. Our chefs' favorite caviar, osetra, is considered to be a more subtle (and less salty) caviar than are either beluga or sevruga, and has a broader range of flavors, from nutty to rich and buttery.

Sevruga caviar comes from the smallest of the sturgeon, which produces the smallest grain eggs, gray black and with a salty taste. The least expensive of the caviars, it is appreciated by some connoisseurs for its singular and identifiable flavor, which can be characterized as a sea essence.

American caviar has only recently been recognized. Many varieties of American sturgeon produce caviar, but the eggs tend to be small and slightly firm. The two types that resemble the Russian pearls most closely are hackleback and paddlefish roe. Hackleback roe is the blackest, and with its salty flavor and slight acidity, is comparable to sevruga. Paddlefish roe is greener in color and has a buttery, nutty flavor similar to that of some osetra caviars. Salmon and trout also produce roe, a bright red orange rather than the classic black. Salmon roe is much larger than trout with a somewhat firmer skin that pops in the mouth to release a more mellow salty flavor. Trout roe is smaller and less flavorful than salmon eggs. American caviar costs *much* less than Russian caviar.

Serving caviar

- Be sure to keep the caviar tins closed and to store them in the coldest part of your refrigerator (but not in the freezer) until you are ready to serve. Opened caviar lasts up to ten days if it is chilled properly. An unopened container will last a month—a good thing for avid romantics to keep on hand.
- To serve caviar, don't offer a metal or silver spoon because they will taint the eggs. Use mother-of-pearl, gold, or bone (even plastic if you must).
- Traditionally, chopped egg yolks and whites, onion, lemon, and sour cream or crème fraîche are served around the tin, and a few toast points finish the platter. But good caviar needs little or no embellishment, tast-

ing quite wonderful when nibbled from on top of the pocket of skin between the thumb joint and the index finger. (That's where they place it during caviar tastings!)

— For occasions of extreme decadence, offer a raw oyster with a drop of sevruga caviar on top (the sevruga has the strongest flavor to match the oyster taste). The flavor is a marvelous combination of sea essence and silky texture.

Champagne: Cupid's Water

Ever since the days of Bacchus and Dionysus, the Greek and Roman gods of wine, ecstasy, and eroticism, wine and spirits have been synonymous with desire. The queen of all wines is champagne. From the sound of the bottle being opened to the shimmering effervescence flowing into a crystal flute, this sparkling wine speaks of celebration and romance. The golden bubbles tickle your tongue, glide down your throat, and go straight to your head, giving the room a rosy glow, making you see stars as you swoon over the person across from you. With all the fanfare and opulence associated with champagne, it is easy to get lost and dazzled among all the choices and subtle differences in the varieties of champagne. So here's a little primer to help you choose and impress your amour with your expertise.

Champagne is the region in France where this famous bubbly was invented. According to the French, only wines made in this region can use this name; wines made by the *méthode champenoise* but that hail from elsewhere should be labeled as sparkling wines. French law does not prevail elsewhere and the two terms are used according to each producer's inclination.

Champagne is made primarily with Chardonnay grapes but other grapes are included to vary the taste and the color. There are three principal types of champagne: demi-sec, wines that are semisweet to sweet; sec, wines that are medium to medium-sweet; and brut, the driest of the wines, though all sparkling wines have some sweetness.

Craving is a common symptom of chocolate addiction. The hankering is remarkably similar to the feeling of divine madness, the longing one experiences when in love. In fact, ever since the Aztecs toasted the gods of fertility with a sacred drink made from the fruits of the cacao tree, people the whole world round have connected love with chocolate.

The process by which the beans of the cacao tree are turned into chocolate is laborious, but nowadays it is easy to procure in various different finished states. As our palate for chocolate has become more refined, supplies of fine chocolate have increased. Gourmet food stores now offer the best chocolate ever. The best dark chocolates have a luster and sheen that is unmistakable; they are flawlessly smooth. Chocolate should have a clean snap when it is broken at room temperature. Good milk chocolate will be less brittle than will its darker counterpart. Like that of a fine wine, the smell ranges from scents of fruit and spice to cedar and tobacco, but the rich, intense aroma of good chocolate is recognizable and can be intoxicating in itself. Whether you prefer sweet milk chocolate or semisweet dark chocolate, the flavors should have balance and the texture be supremely smooth and creamy. Even a Hershey's chocolate kiss meets these standards.

Chocolate used for baking desserts is available in three categories, defined according to the percentage of cocoa solids and the amount of sweetener. Unsweetened chocolate is not sweet at all and, as any finger dipped into a container of cocoa powder will prove, is inedible by itself. Bittersweet chocolate includes some sweetener. Semisweet chocolate is the sweetest of the baking chocolates. (Milk chocolate is not recommended for baking.) The recipes in this cookbook are very specific about the chocolate they require, so read carefully both the recipes and the labels of the chocolate you buy.

Almost all of the chefs we spoke to mentioned chocolate. In fact, this book offers twelve chocolate desserts, a veritable *Kama Sutra* for those of you whose weakness is chocolate. All of these recipes are tried and true, so there's no need to fear even the intricate ones. Just choose your chocolate well, carefully follow the steps outlined in the recipes, and you and your beloved will be astounded with the results.

Love Note: When all else fails, and you can't seem to score any exotic chocolate, rest assured that good old Nestlé's semisweet chocolate chips were used in testing all of the recipes in this book that require semisweet chocolate. The results were stellar. Of course, when we added Ghirardelli's Double Chocolate Chocolate Chips to Nestlé's chips, the desserts were even better. So, 100 percent, expensive chocolate will probably blow you away. We know it would have been too much for us.

Oysters: Bivalves to Boost Your Libido

Dark shells tightly conceal the tantalizing morsels that have been enjoyed for centuries. Offering a fresh taste of the sea, oysters range in flavor from the metallic and salty to the sweet and subtle. Casanova was reported to have eaten over sixty raw oysters a day. Roman emperors imported the vulva-shaped delicacies from England, paying their weight in gold in order to have an abundance of these aphrodisiacs during orgies.

Luckily for us, oysters are farmed and harvested from oyster beds found all around the world, from Nova Scotia to the Chesapeake Bay, from California to Washington State, from Louisiana to Japan and Portugal. The nature of the seawater, the water currents, and the plant life all influence the way these little mollusks taste. These different forces combine to create flavors, textures, and sizes individual to each location. For this reason oysters are named after the place from which they hail. You may still wish to import your oysters from a place far away from your home after you have discovered the nuances of some of the more exotic oysters. Your fishmonger will be able to help you as you consider the many varieties of oysters, directing you toward the sweeter or the saltier ones. Whatever your heart desires . . . there is probably an oyster to satisfy your taste.

The Scoop on Oysters

1. Always buy from a good fishmonger. Oysters should be served on the same day that they are purchased and opened only just before they are served. Be sure to open only the oysters that are firmly closed. Any that are even slightly open should be discarded. When storing oysters in the refrigerator, cover them with a damp cloth but be sure not to submerge in water.

2. To shuck an oyster, first scrub the shell thoroughly under cold running water with a stiff brush. Hold the oyster in a heavy cloth, insert the sharp tip of an oyster knife (a knife with a short strong blade, a pointed tip, and a heavy hand guard at the base of the handle) into the hinge (where the top and bottom shell join). Twist the knife to open the shell, prying it apart with the width of the blade. Then, while pulling at the top shell with the thumb of the hand that is holding the oyster, carefully slide the knife along the inside of the upper shell to cut the muscle that attaches it to the flesh. Pull off and discard the upper shell. Cupping the oyster in your hand so as not to lose the liquid, slide the knife under the oyster meat to free it from the lower shell. Remove any bits of broken shell.

We include several recipes for cooked oysters, but perhaps there is nothing more romantic and enticing than a plate of raw oysters served in their pearly white shells, surrounded by ice, and accompanied by a few wedges of lemon, or cocktail sauce if you prefer. The texture of an oyster as it glides down your throat is exquisite, slippery and creamy at the same time.

With love, nobody really knows what he or she is doing, especially the first time around. Love makes everything new. The best cooking, likewise, comes from the heart. The love and care expended on a meal can be tasted, but there is also some technique involved. All our chefs stressed that simplicity is the key to a romantic meal, but we all know that expertise helps. The following standard procedures will stand you in good stead when attempting any recipe, not just the ones that are intended to seduce.

To blanch vegetables: Bring 2 to 3 quarts of water seasoned with a pinch or two of salt to a boil in a saucepan over high heat. Have ready a large bowl of cold water. When the water boils, drop in the cleaned and trimmed vegetables by handfuls. Cook for about 30 seconds for sugar snap peas or snow peas, a little longer for other vegetables. Be sure to cook until the vegetables are crunch tender and have a bright color. As soon as they are done, remove the vegetables from the hot water and plunge them into the cold water to stop the cooking. Drain and proceed according to the recipe.

Love Note: If holding them for an hour or so, wrap the drained vegetables in paper towels or a clean linen napkin and set them aside to be reheated in the microwave or according to the recipe.

To cut an onion: Cut the onion in half lengthwise using a chef's knife, cutting right through the root end. Using a small paring knife, remove the skin from the top of the onion, leaving the root end intact. Place the onion, cut side down, on a chopping board. With a small knife, make four or five horizontal slits, up to but *not* through the root end. Then make four or five perpendicular cuts, up to but *not* through the root end. Hold the onion together with one hand and, with the other, cut slices from the top of the onion. You will magically have chopped onions with no tears.

To clean leeks: Cut off the dark green tops and the sandy root end and discard. Cut the leek in half lengthwise (unless directed otherwise in the recipe). Holding the root end directly under cold running water, fan out the top portion, allowing the sand to wash out of the leaves. Some chefs rinse off the leeks, cut them first, then soak the chopped part in cold water. When soaking leeks, be sure to let them stand for at least 20 minutes to allow the sand to fall to the bottom of the pan. Then carefully remove the leeks with your hands, transfer them to a colander to rinse them under cold water once more, and then drain well.

To make chocolate shavings: Shave a chocolate bar or chocolate chunk with a vegetable peeler, running it along the flat side of the chocolate. This works equally well for white and dark chocolate.

To make confit of garlic: Preheat the oven to 250°F. Peel a whole head of garlic, keeping the cloves whole. Place the garlic in a small ovenproof container and cover with olive oil. Cover the container with foil and bake until the garlic is tender to the point of a knife but still holds its shape and remains uncolored, about 1 hour.

To make toast points for caviar: Preheat the oven to 350°F. Cut the crusts off thin slices of white bread. Cut each slice diagonally to create two triangles. Arrange the bread on ungreased baking sheets and bake until the bread becomes light brown on the edges, turning the slices over after about 8 minutes; the total baking time is 10 to 15 minutes. Store in an airtight container.

To prepare asparagus: Wash the fresh asparagus in cold water. Hold on to the tip end with one hand and use a vegetable peeler to peel the asparagus from top to bottom. Dip the tip end of the spear in cold water to soak until all the spears are peeled. Break off the woody bottom part and then trim the end with a sharp knife so that all the spears are the same length.

To roast beets: Cut off the beet leaves about 1½ inches from the bulb. Wash, but do not peel, the beet and leave the root intact. Wrap the beet in a sheet of aluminum foil, sealing it into a small package. Roast the beet in a preheated 425°F oven until tender to the point of a fork, about 45 minutes, depending on the size of the beet. Cool the beet until you are able to handle it, slip off the skin, and proceed according to the recipe.

To roast garlic: Norman Van Aken of Norman's in Coral Gables rubs the head of garlic with olive oil; others wrap the garlic in aluminum foil; yet others just roast it dry. No matter which method you choose, garlic is always roasted unpeeled. Preheat the oven to 400°F. Place the garlic on a baking pan and roast until the skin is golden brown and the cloves are soft inside. A whole head will take about 1 hour; individual cloves will take 20 to 30 minutes.

Love Note: When sautéing garlic, watch carefully. Because of the high sugar content, garlic burns easily; cook it until soft.

To roast a pepper: Preheat the oven to 400°F. Rub the pepper with olive oil, place it on a baking sheet, and roast until charred and soft, 20 to 25 minutes. Remove the pepper from the oven and place it in a paper bag. Let rest for 5 minutes. Remove the pepper, pull off the skin, cut in half, and remove the seeds. Pat dry with paper towels and proceed according to the recipe.

To toast nuts: Heat a small dry skillet over high heat, add the nuts, and shake the pan vigorously and constantly until the nuts become aromatic and light brown, 2 or 3 minutes. Immediately tip the nuts out of the skillet onto paper towels and let them cool. Sprinkle with a pinch of coarse salt for savory dishes.

To segment citrus fruit: Work over a mixing bowl to catch the juices. Cut off the peel and pith from the fruit, exposing the segments. Cut down on either side of the membrane that separates the segments and release them. Discard the peel and membrane.

To toast spices: Heat a small dry skillet over high heat, add the spice, and shake the pan constantly until the spice becomes aromatic, 1 to 2 minutes. Immediately remove from the skillet.

To trim a scallop: Using a very sharp knife, remove the tiny, tough, opaque-looking muscle that is attached to the side of each scallop. Rinse and pat the scallop dry, then proceed according to the recipe.

To improvise a double boiler: Fill a 2-quart saucepan about one-third full of water, set it over moderately high heat, and bring the water to a simmer. Place a stainless steel bowl on top of the saucepan and you have a double boiler.

Happily Ever After

Here are sweet but simple recipes to complete your romantic evenings.

Whipped Cream

1 cup heavy cream, cold
2 to 3 tablespoons powdered sugar

1 teaspoon pure vanilla extract

CHILL THE bowl and beaters before whipping. In a mixing bowl, whip the cream with beaters or a wire whisk until soft peaks form. Slowly add the sugar and vanilla and continue beating until the cream is stiff. (If it's warm in your kitchen, place the mixing bowl over another bowl filled with ice.) Refrigerate if not serving immediately.

Yield: Makes about 2 cups

Love Note: To vary the flavor, add 1 teaspoon almond extract or the grated rind of half a lemon, orange, or lime, or ½ teaspoon cinnamon.

Put away the Cool

Whip and discard that can of Reddi-wip! The full flavor of the real thing is one of the luxuries that sensuous dining demands.

—

Crème Fraîche

1 cup heavy cream   1 cup sour cream

IN A medium mixing bowl, whisk the heavy and sour cream together. Cover with plastic wrap and let stand at room temperature for 4 to 6 hours. Transfer to a clean container and refrigerate. Will keep for up to 2 weeks in the refrigerator.

Yield: Makes 2 cups

Crème fraîche is like a little black dress: You can dress it up, dress it down; it works for savory as well as sweet foods. As a substitute for whipped cream or ice cream, it provides a silky smooth sensation on the tongue that is perfect to top off a goblet half filled with berries for dessert or breakfast.

—

Yogurt Cheese

1 pint nonfat plain yogurt

1 EMPTY THE yogurt into a yogurt strainer or a sieve set over a bowl and lined with damp cheesecloth or linen napkin. Cover the whole affair with plastic wrap and refrigerate overnight. The next day, transfer the yogurt cheese (curd) to a clean container, discard the liquid (whey), and refrigerate. Will keep, refrigerated, for up to 2 weeks.

2 FOR TWO servings, spoon out about ¼ cup of the yogurt cheese into a small bowl. Whisk in a very little sweetener (honey, artificial sweetener, or sugar to taste) and a drop of two of vanilla or pure almond extract. Grated zest of lemon, orange, or lime works well, too. Taste and correct the flavoring. Use as a topping on cake, tarts, or fruit.

Yield: Makes about 1 cup

Chocolate Sauce

14 ounces chocolate, the best quality
    you can find, cut into chunks (use
    12 ounces semisweet and 2 ounces
    unsweetened chocolate for a deep
    rich flavor)

1½ cups heavy cream
1 tablespoon pure vanilla extract

1 MELT THE chocolate in a stainless steel mixing bowl set over (but not touching) simmering water in a saucepan. Stir until the chocolate is smooth.

2 USING A wire whisk, add the heavy cream in a steady stream, whisking constantly until it is well incorporated. The chocolate may "seize" (become lumpy) for a moment or two. Do not despair! Continue whisking and adding the cream gradually and the sauce will become satiny smooth. Stir in the vanilla, taste, and adjust the flavoring. This may be made ahead and refrigerated for up to 1 month.

3 TO SERVE, reheat in a small bowl set over a pan of barely simmering water.

Yield: Makes about 2½ cups

> This elegant sauce has only two ingredients (and a little vanilla if you want), is simple to prepare, and keeps for ages . . . just like love.

Apricot Glaze

½ cup apricot jam
1 to 2 tablespoons water or liqueur,
   such as kirsch

1 MELT THE jam with the water or liqueur in a small saucepan set over high heat (about 4 minutes) or in a small, glass microwave-proof container (about 1 minute). Stir until blended and then press through a fine sieve.
2 TO USE, dip a very clean pastry brush into the glaze. Generously and gently brush the glaze over each piece or slice of fruit. To set the glaze up quickly, refrigerate the painted dessert for about 10 minutes.

Yield: Makes ½ cup

Simple Syrup

½ cup sugar

¼ cup water

1 teaspoon pure vanilla extract

IN A medium saucepan set over high heat, combine the sugar and water and bring to a boil. Add the vanilla and cook for 2 minutes. Remove from the heat and let cool. Store in a clean, airtight container and refrigerate for up to 2 weeks.

Yield: Makes about ½ cup

This cooked sugar solution is used as a glaze and for soaking cakes, preserving fruit, and as the basis for many candies.

Simple Brown Sauce

1 tablespoon unsalted butter

½ medium onion, chopped

¼ cup chopped celery

¼ cup chopped carrots

1 tablespoon all-purpose flour

3 cups beef stock, boiling

2 tablespoons tomato paste

1 bay leaf

Salt and freshly ground black pepper

1 IN A nonreactive heavy saucepan over medium-high heat, melt the butter and cook the vegetables, stirring, until the onions are soft and translucent, about 4 minutes.

2 ADD THE flour and cook, stirring constantly, until the flour becomes aromatic, about 2 minutes.

3 WHISK IN the hot stock and continue stirring until well mixed. Whisk in the tomato paste, then add the bay leaf and salt and pepper to taste. Simmer for 30 minutes.

4 STRAIN THE sauce through a fine-mesh sieve, taste, and correct the seasonings.

5 COOL TO room temperature. Transfer to an airtight container, cover, and refrigerate for up to 1 week, or freeze for up to 1 month.

Yield: Makes 2½ cups

As she strode out of the elevator, I whispered to myself, "I must get to know this woman." Her copper hair and ivory skin had infused me with rising passion. "Pardon me," I said. "Didn't you want the first floor?" "Oh yes! You're right. I do want the first floor."

As the car reached the ground floor, she turned to me and said, "Thank you." Our eyes met for the first time—hers radiating a startling emerald green with a fleck of gold. "You work up on eight, don't you?" I asked. I'd noticed her before. "Yes," she said, "in the court. I'm a deputy district attorney." She smiled and strode away.

When I called the D.A.'s office to ask the name of the deputy district attorney, she answered the phone. "My name is Mary K. and, yes, I remember you from the elevator." I introduced myself as Sam A. and invited her to coffee some morning. After a moment's hesitation, she replied, "How is tomorrow morning?"

A fast romance sprang up. Within two weeks, we were in love. "Valentine's Day is approaching. Write me onto your calendar for the fourteenth," I begged.

The table was set with a white tablecloth, red napkins, tall candles, and early spring flowers. Mary was magnificent. Her long burnished copper hair swept back from her forehead and down over her back like a great waterfall. We supped, drank, and tasted every morsel of every dish. Afterward, we stretched out on the deep leather sofa in the den. I held her, kissed her, and turned out the light. What a wonderful supper we'd had!

Love,
Sam

Sam Arnold

The Fort

Denver, Colorado

Menu

Champagne—Moët & Chandon White Star

Martha Washington's Chicken Breast

Rice Pilaf with Quinoa and Barberries

French Pinot Noir—Sancerre, Loire Valley (served chilled)

Mixed Green Salad with Herb Vinaigrette and Croutons

Chocolate Negrita

Martha Washington's Chicken Breasts

Two 6- to 8-ounce boneless skinless chicken breasts
1 cup chicken stock
1 tablespoon vegetable oil
1 shallot, minced
¼ cup *verjus* (see Love Note)
¼ cup sugar

1 tablespoon cornstarch dissolved in 2 tablespoons cold water
1 tablespoon butter
½ teaspoon freshly ground black pepper
Salt

1 PLACE THE chicken breasts and enough chicken stock to cover in a medium saucepan set over high heat. Bring to a boil, then remove from the heat, cover, and set aside until the breasts are perfectly poached, about 12 minutes. Pour off the stock, reserving about ½ cup.

2 ADD THE oil to a skillet set over medium-high heat and cook the shallot, stirring, until soft and translucent, 1 to 2 minutes. Add the *verjus,* sugar, and reserved stock and whisk together. Slowly whisk the cornstarch mixture into the sauce to thicken. Simmer, stirring often, until the sauce lightly coats the back of a spoon, is reduced, and has a pleasant, sweet-and-sour taste with an onion base, 4 to 5 minutes.

3 WHILE THE sauce simmers, rub the warm chicken breasts with a dot of butter on both sides, sprinkle with pepper, and add salt to taste. Place the chicken breasts in the sauce and reheat for about 4 minutes.

Love Note: Verjus, commonly used during medieval and Renaissance times, is a sour, acidic liquid made from unripe fruit, usually grapes. It is available in gourmet groceries. A combination of ⅛ cup lemon juice and ⅛ cup orange juice is an easy substitution.

Rice Pilaf with Quinoa and Barberries

½ cup basmati rice

2 cups water

4 strands saffron

¼ cup dried currants

1 tablespoon barberries or dried
    cranberries

½ cup quinoa

2 tablespoons pine nuts

2 tablespoons finely diced red bell
    pepper

2 tablespoons finely diced green bell
    pepper

2 to 3 tablespoons extra virgin olive oil

Salt and freshly ground black pepper

3 or 4 cilantro sprigs, for garnish

Half a red bell pepper, sliced, for
    garnish

Quinoa, a small grain rich in protein and calcium, and sweet barberries add nutrients and flavor to this aromatic and nutty rice mixture. Washing it rinses off the slightly soapy dust quinoa has and improves its taste.

1 WASH THE rice in cold water, changing the water (as many as six times) until it is no longer cloudy, and drain well. Place the washed rice, 1 cup of the water, the saffron, currants, and barberries in a heavy saucepan with a lid. Bring to a boil, uncovered. Cover, turn off the heat, and let the rice steam for 10 minutes. Uncover and fluff the rice with a fork. Set aside.

2 WASH THE quinoa in a fine-mesh strainer, pushing your hand back and forth in it as the water pours through. Place the rinsed quinoa in 1 cup of water with ¼ teaspoon salt in a heavy saucepan over high heat and cook it only until it is soft and the grains are swollen, about 10 minutes.

3 TOAST THE pine nuts (see page 12) and set aside.

4 EMPTY THE rice and quinoa into a large bowl. Using chopsticks or 2 forks, gently toss the pine nuts, diced peppers, and olive oil into the grains. (The heat will soften the peppers.) Season to taste with salt and pepper.

5 SPOON A serving of the rice pilaf onto each warm dinner plate; place the chicken on top and spoon the sauce over the whole affair. Garnish with sprigs of cilantro and red pepper slices for color.

Chocolate Negrita

¾ pound Ghirardelli semisweet dark
    chocolate, cut into chunks
3 large eggs, pasteurized
Salt

2 teaspoons pure vanilla extract
2 tablespoons Myers's dark rum
Whipped Cream (see page 14), for
    topping

1 MELT THE chocolate in a double boiler (see page 13 for an improvisation). When the chocolate is half melted, turn off the heat and let the chocolate continue to melt and keep warm.

2 SEPARATE THE eggs. Beat the egg whites with a pinch of salt until stiff.

3 IN ANOTHER mixing bowl, beat the egg yolks until they are pale yellow and a ribbon forms when the beaters are lifted. In a slow stream, with the beaters running, add the warm chocolate, mixing thoroughly. Beat in the vanilla and rum. Fold the beaten egg whites into the yolk mixture until thoroughly blended.

4 LADLE THE Negrita into 4 large wineglasses or pretty goblets. Refrigerate until serving time.

5 TO SERVE, pipe a rosette of vanilla-flavored whipped cream on top of each Negrita and set the glasses on a doily-lined plate.

"Cooking for me," said Carmello Barillo, "is like making love. You have to put the same passion and tension into it." The Sicilian-born chef must have some very satisfied customers at Fiorello's Roman Café. Across from Lincoln Center in Manhattan, the restaurant offers an antipasto bar overflowing with Mediterranean seafood and vegetable salads. In the summertime, crowds flock to the outdoor café for fruity gelati and sundaes.

The evening he moved in with a former girlfriend, Carmello decided to surprise her with dinner. He picked up some ingredients at the local market, dug through his boxes to find two pans, and made eggplant Parmesan and baked a striped bass. Sitting on the floor, they dined off a cardboard box covered with a cloth and set with candles. "It was one of the most romantic evenings we spent together."

The relationship has ended but the memory stays. In a thick Italian accent he says, "There weren't bad feeling when we broke up. I still love her and she loves me. But I don't think of going back, only forward. Maybe it's because I'm Sicilian."

The preparation for the eggplant and fish can be done earlier in the day. When you are finished, take a long hot bath and get dressed. Assemble the strawberries and break open the champagne. Pour a glass for yourself and add a splash to the berries. Place them in the refrigerator. When your heartthrob arrives, pop the eggplant dish into the oven and settle in the living room for another glass of champagne. Take out the eggplant and put the fish into the oven. Don't forget to set the timer! By the time you finish the first course, the fish will be done and ready to be presented on a beautiful platter.

Carmello Barillo

Fiorello's Roman Café

New York

Menu

Champagne—Moët & Chandon

Baked Eggplant with Ricotta and Tomatoes

Baked Striped Bass

California Sauvignon Blanc

Macerated Strawberries

Espresso

Baked Eggplant with Ricotta and Tomatoes

When the weather gets chilly, tender slices of eggplant blanketed in creamy ricotta cheese and rich tomato sauce make a hearty starter. If tomatoes are not in season, you can substitute 8 ounces canned whole peeled tomatoes

—

Olive oil

2 large tomatoes, peeled and seeded

1 clove garlic, peeled

6 to 8 basil leaves (2 left whole, 5 cut into slivers)

Salt and freshly ground black pepper

1 small eggplant

½ cup ricotta cheese

1 large egg yolk

2 tablespoons freshly grated Parmesan cheese

Extra virgin olive oil for drizzling

1 COAT THE bottom of a small saucepan set over moderate heat with a film of olive oil, add the tomato, garlic, and the 2 whole basil leaves, and season to taste with salt and pepper. Bring the mixture to a simmer and cook until thickened, stirring occasionally, about 8 minutes. Remove from the heat and set aside.

2 SLICE THE eggplant lengthwise into 6 or 7 long, ½-inch-thick pieces and pat them dry with paper towels.

3 COAT THE bottom of a large nonstick skillet set over moderately high heat with a film of oil, add the eggplant, and cook until golden brown, about 3 minutes per side. Transfer the eggplant to a baking sheet lined with paper towels and set aside.

4 IN A mixing bowl, mix the ricotta with the egg yolk, 4 of the slivered basil leaves, 1 tablespoon of the Parmesan, and salt and pepper to taste.

5 PREHEAT THE oven to 375°F. Lightly oil a medium-size, pretty oven-to-table dish that will hold the eggplant in one layer.

6 WORKING ON a flat surface, evenly distribute the cheese over each slice of eggplant, roll the slices up, and place them, seam side down, in the baking dish. Spoon the tomato sauce on top and sprinkle with the remaining tablespoon of Parmesan cheese.

7 BAKE UNTIL golden brown on top, about 20 minutes. Garnish with the slivered basil and serve from the baking dish.

Baked Striped Bass

One 14- to 16-ounce whole striped
  bass, scaled and boned, except for
  the spine, with head and tail intact
3 cloves garlic, peeled
1 small bunch Italian or flat-leaf
  parsley, stems discarded
2 pinches crushed red pepper flakes

Sea salt
3 tablespoons extra virgin olive oil
1 lemon, washed, cut into 6 thin
  circles, seeds removed
¾ to 1 cup dry white wine
Freshly ground black pepper
Flat-leaf parsley sprigs, for garnish

The succulence of striped bass is unparalleled and the simple preparation of this elegant fish allows the light flavor to shine.

—

1 PREHEAT THE oven to 375°F. Lightly coat with oil a nonreactive baking pan that will accommodate the fish. Wash the fish in cold water and pat it dry with paper towels.

2 CHOP THE garlic and parsley leaves together with the red pepper flakes and 2 or 3 pinches of salt until finely minced. Transfer to a small bowl and add 2 tablespoons of the olive oil.

3 SPREAD THE parsley mixture inside the cavity of the fish. Place the lemon slices inside the fish and transfer the fish to a lightly oiled baking pan.

4 POUR THE wine and a splash of water over the fish. Season with salt and pepper to taste and drizzle the remaining tablespoon of olive oil over. Bake until the fish is firm to the touch; the center should flake to the point of a knife and turn opaque, about 17 minutes.

5 TRANSFER THE fish to a pretty platter, garnish with sprigs of flat-leaf parsley, and serve at the table.

Macerated Strawberries

It's hard to imagine an improvement on fresh strawberries, but this cold marinade of berries certainly ups the ante to almost ambrosial levels. Raspberry sorbet with orange and vanilla adds a rich piquancy that rounds out the wonder of the fresh berries.

1 scoop raspberry sorbet

Juice of half a lemon

Juice of half an orange

1 tablespoon sugar

2 tablespoons Grand Marnier liqueur

Splash of champagne

Half a vanilla bean

1 pint fresh strawberries, washed, stemmed, and quartered

½ cup heavy cream, whipped (see page 14)

1 STIR THE sorbet together with the lemon and orange juices. Add the sugar, the liqueur, and champagne. Cut the bean in half lengthwise and scrape the seeds into the sorbet.

2 FOLD THE berries into the sorbet mixture and mix well. Divide the berries between two large wineglasses or spoon them all into a large beautiful cut-glass bowl, cover with plastic wrap, and refrigerate for at least 15 minutes.

3 GARNISH THE strawberries with whipped cream and serve.

"For me," declares Lidia Bastianich, New York City's matriarch of Italian cuisine, "food is an expression of my love and creativity. It's something that you can take into your body besides sex." At Felidia, she expresses her passion through hearty risottos, fresh fish, and pillows of stuffed pasta. One woman was recently overheard moaning, "Oh, my god, yes, yes!" after her date fed her a spoonful of creamy wild mushroom risotto.

Ecstasy is no further than your own kitchen if you prepare Lidia's recipes. "This is a sensual meal that caresses you with warmth for what might follow," Lidia hints. What she likes about home-cooked romance is the fun and games that couples can share. Begin the foreplay in the kitchen where you can tie an apron around his waist, kissing his neck as you do. Eating out of one bowl, gently lay spoonfuls of risotto into each others' mouths. After dinner, blindfold your date and feed him an assortment of goodies such as chocolate, whipped cream, honey—*9½ Weeks* style. Don't forget to give him a kiss for each flavor he identifies correctly!

Lidia Matticchio
Bastianich

Felidia

New York

Menu

Bruschetta with Tuscan Beans and Caviar

Risotto with Wild Mushrooms

Italian Barbaresco, Bruno Giacosa, 1982

Chocolate Zabaglione Sauce with Fresh Berries

Bruschetta with Tuscan Beans and Caviar

Ricchi e poveri
(the rich and the poor)
meet in this dish to
create a tasty, elegant,
and mellow flavor.
Allow enough time,
about one hour after
cooking, for the beans
to come to room
temperature.

¾ cup (¼ pound) dried *cannellini*, or
use baby lima or Great Northern
beans, picked over
1 bay leaf
1 clove garlic, crushed
1½ tablespoons extra virgin olive oil
1 tablespoon minced red onion
1 hard-boiled egg, white and yolk
chopped separately

1 ounce good-quality caviar, beluga,
osetra, or American sturgeon
Freshly ground black pepper
½ cup small, tender salad greens,
washed and spun dry
6 slices Italian bread, cut ½ inch thick,
drizzled with olive oil, and toasted

1 PLACE THE beans in a medium-size bowl and pour enough cold water over them to cover by 4 inches. Soak in a cool place for at least 8 hours or overnight.

2 DRAIN THE beans and discard the soaking water. In a large heavy saucepan set over high heat, combine the beans with enough fresh cold water to cover generously and add the bay leaf and garlic. Bring to a boil, reduce the heat, and simmer until tender, about 30 minutes.

3 DRAIN THE beans and remove the bay leaf and garlic. Transfer to a mixing bowl and toss the beans with olive oil and let them stand, tossing occasionally, until they are lukewarm, about 30 minutes.

4 GENTLY FOLD the onion, chopped egg, and caviar into the beans. Season to taste with pepper. Drizzle a bit of extra virgin olive oil over the salad greens.

5 FOR EACH serving, arrange 3 slices of toasted bread on a pretty plate, divide the bean mixture evenly among the slices, mound a few greens in the center of the plate, and serve at once.

Risotto with Wild Mushrooms

For the mushrooms

2 tablespoons dry *porcini* mushrooms

¼ cup hot chicken stock

6 ounces fresh wild mushrooms (black
trumpet, shiitake, chanterelles,
etc.)

1 tablespoon olive oil

¼ teaspoon salt

For the risotto

1½ tablespoons olive oil

½ cup minced onions

1 shallot (1 tablespoon) minced

1 cup Arborio rice

½ cup dry white wine

3 cups good chicken stock, simmering

2 tablespoons butter, cut into pieces

½ cup freshly grated Parmesan cheese

Salt and freshly ground black pepper

> **Transforming**
> Arborio rice into
> warm creamy risotto
> takes a lot of stirring.
> But it's worth it,
> especially for this dish.
> The robust flavor of
> wild mushrooms will
> soothe and satisfy

1 RINSE THE dry *porcini* to remove any dirt. Soak the mushrooms in the hot chicken stock in a small bowl for 20 minutes.

2 TRIM AND discard the woody parts of the wild mushrooms, wash, and pat dry on paper towels. Cut the mushrooms lengthwise into ½-inch slices.

3 COAT WITH oil the bottom of a medium skillet; set over high heat. When the oil smokes, toss in the mushrooms and salt, and cook, shaking the pan constantly, to evaporate the moisture and intensify the flavor, about 5 minutes.

4 TO PREPARE the risotto, invite your guest into the kitchen and share some wine while you take turns stirring. Coat with oil the bottom of a heavy-bottomed, medium saucepan; set over high heat. Add the onions and cook, stirring, until translucent, about 2 minutes. Add the shallot and cook, stirring, for about 1 minute. Reduce the heat to medium high and stir the rice into the onion mixture rather slowly and constantly until the grains turn golden and feel loose and dry. "They will click softly in the pan." Raise the heat to high, add the wine, and boil it down. When the rice is almost dry, ladle in enough hot stock to barely cover the rice. Regulate the heat so that the stock just simmers. Stir constantly and slowly from now on.

5 CONTINUE ADDING chicken stock as the rice absorbs it. After the rice has been cooking for about 8 minutes, stir in the sautéed wild mushrooms. Ladle about ¼ cup of stock into the sauté pan to deglaze it and pour the liquid into the risotto. Keep stirring the risotto. Remove the soaked *porcini* and squeeze their juices back into the bowl. Chop the soaked mushrooms and stir them into the risotto. Strain the soaking water of any sand and sediment and pour it into the risotto.

6 WHEN THE grains have doubled in size, are suspended in a creamy liquid, and are just tender, *al dente,* remove the risotto from the heat. Stir in the butter and half of the cheese with a wooden spoon and season with salt and pepper to taste. Immediately transfer the risotto to warmed soup plates, sprinkle with Parmesan cheese, and serve at once. Pass the remaining cheese at the table.

Chocolate Zabaglione Sauce

3 egg yolks at room temperature

3 tablespoons dry marsala

3 tablespoons sugar

1½ ounces semisweet chocolate, chopped and melted

1 IN A large saucepan, bring 3 inches of water to a simmer.

2 IN A large copper or very clean stainless-steel bowl, whisk together the egg yolks, marsala, and sugar. Set the bowl over the saucepan of simmering water and whisk constantly until the mixture is fluffy, light, and hot, about 4 minutes.

3 REMOVE FROM the heat. And very slowly fold in the melted chocolate. Serve at once in a wide bowl and accompany with berries and squares of pound cake.

At Felidia, Chef Bastianich serves a *Torta di zabaglione al cioccolata* (chocolate zabaglione cake) for dessert. The rich chocolate sauce that accompanies this cake makes a terrific fondue, perfect for dipping pound cake, fresh berries, or fingers. It's a bit tricky but worth the risk.

➝

Vincent Bommarito, Jr.

Tony's

Saint Louis, Missouri

NIGHT AFTER NIGHT, Vincent Bommarito, Jr., does his father proud, cranking out Italian-fare favorites at Tony's, the family's five-star restaurant in Saint Louis. But on his nights off, the chef is just as happy to pick up his date and visit some other family's restaurant. "It's nice to get waited on for a change."

According to Vincent, by the fourth or fifth date, he is usually ready to invite her to a home-cooked meal. "I like to make homey foods that aren't confusing to understand. And besides, everybody likes pasta," he says.

His advice to budding chefs is simple. "If you screw up something, throw it out and try again. Just keep plugging." The rewards for slaving away at the stove are great. "If the evening is a success, next time you can eat in front of the TV and forget all the romantic stuff!"

Menu

Broccoli Salad with Red Pepper, Onion, and Black Olives

Pasta with Fresh Tomato, Basil, Arugula, and Mozzarella

Italian Chardonnay—Dreams Jermann (1995)

Strawberries with Balsamic Vinegar

➤

Broccoli Salad with Red Pepper, Onion, and Black Olives

½ head broccoli, cut into 2-inch
    florets
3 tablespoons olive oil
1 tablespoon red wine vinegar
¼ cup chopped red onion

½ red bell pepper, roasted (page 12),
    peeled, seeded, and finely chopped
12 Italian black olives, cut in half and
    pitted
Salt and freshly ground black pepper

1 IN A steamer or a colander placed over boiling water, steam the broccoli florets until bright green and tender but still crunchy, about 4 minutes. Do not overcook. Immediately plunge into cold water, drain well, and refrigerate.

2 IN A small mixing bowl, whisk together the olive oil and vinegar. Mix in the onion, red pepper, and olives. Add the cold broccoli and toss to combine. Refrigerate for 2 hours. Adjust the seasoning with salt and pepper to taste. Mound on a salad plate and serve cold.

For your favorite vegetable lover, the combination of crunchy broccoli with red peppers and olives is as beautiful as it is delicious.

Pasta with Fresh Tomato, Basil, Arugula, and Mozzarella

2 tablespoons olive oil
Half an onion, minced
5 ripe, firm tomatoes, peeled (see Love
    Note), seeded, and chopped, with
    their juices reserved
2 to 3 tablespoons chopped fresh basil

Salt and freshly ground black pepper
¾ pound pasta, your choice
1 cup mozzarella, cut into medium-
    size cubes
1 cup julienned arugula

1 COAT WITH oil the bottom of a large saucepan; set over medium-high heat. Add the onion and cook, stirring, until it becomes soft and translucent, about 3 minutes.

2 ADD THE tomatoes and basil. Stir well and bring to a boil. Reduce the heat and simmer until most of the liquid has cooked from the tomatoes, 15 to 20 minutes. Season with salt and pepper to taste.

3 COOK THE pasta according to directions. Drain well and toss with the sauce and cheese. Serve the pasta at once in warm soup bowls or plates with the arugula sprinkled over the top.

Love Note: To peel tomatoes, drop them into boiling water for 30 seconds. The skins should then slip off easily.

Strawberries with Balsamic Vinegar

1 pint ripe strawberries

2 tablespoons good balsamic vinegar

1 tablespoon superfine sugar

1 teaspoon grated orange zest

1 WASH AND hull the berries, quarter them, add the balsamic vinegar, and marinate for 15 to 20 minutes

2 COMBINE THE sugar and zest and sprinkle over the berries. Mix well and serve in pretty goblets.

Vinegar on berries? Yes! The acidity of the vinegar draws out the sweetness of the berries. The orange zest pulls the two tastes together.

At Lex Chutintaranoid's charming bistro in Ithaca, New York, the triangular tables are small for a reason: His guests' knees should be touching. "People complain, but once they sit down, they'll stay for hours," he says. "It's better when you are face to face—you don't get distracted by other people." His new wife Phoebe agrees. "They are really great 'date' tables."

Lex has made his bride weak in the knees ever since they first met while she was working as a waitress in a local Japanese restaurant. Phoebe, who was nervous about waiting on the famous restaurateur, flubbed his order. But Lex fell head over heels for Phoebe anyway, even snagging an invitation to the restaurant's Christmas party so that he could see her again. Phoebe quickly found herself swept away. "Lex is like a pomegranate," she says. "A hard shell on the outside with beautiful little jewels on the inside."

At their restaurant, Lex lets his softer side show in his savory East-meets-West cuisine. "It unintentionally symbolizes Lex and me," Phoebe explains. "Lex is from Thailand and I'm from the United States."

If you can't make it to Ithaca this year, this sailor's feast will tide you over. "For Lex," says Phoebe, "the sea is a very sensual and romantic thing, and so anything from the sea has that feeling to it. I suspect a date would be very impressed if you were to bring these beautiful dishes to the table."

Menu

Stuffed Soft-Shell Crab

Herman J. Wiemer Dry Riesling

Chilean Sea Bass with Coconut and Pine-Nut Sauce over *Capellini*

Alsace–Mittnacht-Klack, Gewürztraminer, 1996

Fresh Apricots Dipped in Warm Chocolate Sauce

Stuffed Soft-Shell Crabs

3 tablespoons Chinese fermented
   salted black beans, rinsed
Sake or dry sherry to cover the beans
2 tablespoons extra virgin olive oil
1 clove garlic, minced
1 tablespoon minced fresh ginger
1 jalapeño pepper, roasted (page 12),
   seeds and skin removed, and
   minced
¼ cup diced water chestnuts
¼ cup minced fresh cilantro

¼ cup bread crumbs, divided
¼ cup freshly grated Parmesan cheese
2 large soft-shell crabs, cleaned
   (ask the fishmonger to do this)
Flour for dredging
1 large egg
Vegetable oil for frying
2 large leaves red-leaf or Boston
   lettuce, for serving
Thai *sri racha* (chile-and-garlic) sauce
   or other thick chile sauce

1 RINSE THE black beans in water several times, drain well, and let them dry on a paper towel. Then in a small bowl soak the beans in the sake for 1 hour.

2 SET A small skillet over medium heat, add the olive oil, then the garlic and ginger, and cook until the garlic is light brown, about 4 minutes. Remove the pan from the heat, stir in the jalapeño pepper, water chestnuts, cilantro, 2 tablespoons of the bread crumbs, and the cheese and mix well. Transfer the mixture to a bowl and set aside or cover and refrigerate.

3 TO PREPARE the crab, use scissors to cut around the front of the shell, toward the eyes, cutting only enough to lift the top of the shell slightly. Gather up a small handful of stuffing, pat it into a ball, stuff it underneath the shell of the crab, and lightly flatten to distribute. Replace the shell.

4 ON A shallow plate, place enough flour to cover the bottom about ¼ inch deep. In another shallow bowl or plate, beat the egg lightly with 3 tablespoons of water. Place the remaining 2 tablespoons of bread crumbs on

The crunchy outer shell of these crabs is just a prelude to the smooth silky undersides. Add to that the fresh-tasting stuffing and you have an incredibly sexy appetizer that could stand alone for dinner when served with a simple green salad and fresh berries for dessert.

a third plate. First, dip each crab in the flour to coat it lightly and tap off the excess flour. Then, dip the crab in the egg mixture and then roll it in the bread crumbs, coating it thoroughly, and set aside.

5 IF YOU have a deep fryer, fry the crabs until they are light brown in color, about 4 minutes. Or, set a frying pan over medium-high heat, add about ½ inch vegetable oil to the pan, and heat the oil until it shimmers. (To test, toss a few bread crumbs on the oil; they should brown quickly.) Add the crabs and fry until they are light brown on both sides, about 3 minutes per side. Transfer the crabs to paper towels to drain. To serve, place them on large red-leaf or Boston lettuce leaves and pass the Thai *sri racha* or chile sauce at the table.

Chilean Sea Bass with Coconut and Pine-Nut Sauce over *Capellini*

For the marinade

¼ cup light soy sauce

1 teaspoon fresh lime juice

Two 6- to 7-ounce Chilean sea
   bass fillets

1 tablespoon finely minced fresh
   lemongrass

1 cup pine nuts, toasted (see page 12)

For the sauce

3 tablespoons Thai shrimp and chile
   paste (Lan Chi brand)

One 13½-ounce can coconut milk

1 minced kaffir lime leaf, or grated
   zest of half a lime

1 tablespoon finely minced fresh
   lemongrass

3 to 4 tablespoons fresh squeezed lime
   juice or tamarind juice

1 tablespoon Thai fish sauce (*nam pla*)

½ pound dried *capellini*, cooked
   according to package directions

The fresh citrus marinade gently scents the firm bass that is then grilled, served on a bed of pasta, and dressed up with coconut milk sauce. Simple to execute, this subtle dish is suited to a fish lover.

1 TO MAKE the marinade, whisk together the soy sauce, lime juice, and lemongrass in a small bowl. Place the sea bass in a shallow pan, cover with the marinade, cover with plastic, and marinate for 1 hour.

2 TOAST THE pine nuts, measure out ⅓ cup, and set them aside. Chop the rest coarsely; you should have about ½ cup when chopped.

3 TO MAKE the sauce, combine the chile paste, coconut milk, lime leaf, lemongrass, lime juice, and fish sauce in a small saucepan set over moderately high heat. Bring to a boil, reduce the heat, and add the chopped pine nuts. Simmer together for 3 minutes and remove from the heat.

4 PREHEAT THE broiler or grill to high. Broil or grill the fish until the flesh turns from translucent to opaque, 5 to 10 minutes per inch of thickness.

5 MOUND THE pasta on two warm plates, set the bass on top, and generously ladle the sauce over the fish. Garnish with the whole pine nuts.

Ann Cooper

The Putney Inn

Putney, Vermont

A BRICK HEARTH AND decorative antiques give a romantic flavor to the dining room of the seventeenth-century farmhouse that is now The Putney Inn. After a dinner of local favorites such as smoked Cheddar chowder, New England sole with cornmeal crust, or roast turkey breast with maple-pecan stuffing, guests can stroll down to the river, explore wildflowers, or simply return to their rooms. On Valentine's Day at the inn, Cooper pulls out all the stops, preparing Maine lobster chèvre pillows, spinach-stuffed roasted leg of lamb, and small flourless chocolate cakes. "The lamb is served on one plate so that couples can feed each other. And the cake has just enough sugar to keep you up for whatever happens in the hours to come.

"It's a very special thing to feed someone, whether it's a child, a friend, or a lover," says Ann. "It's something that you are creating with your own hands." To create an ambience for any sensuous supper, the chef suggests playing jazz and dimming the lights.

Ann enjoys preparing other kinds of meals. "I've shared some very intimate but simple picnics. Drinking some wine, eating cheese and bread. It doesn't have to be a big deal to be amorous." Once, she and a boyfriend were swimming in Vancouver when they discovered oysters a few feet down. They collected a bucketful, picked up a pound of butter, and cooked the oysters over an open fire on the beach.

The real secret to a successful relationship isn't just in the food. For Ann, honest communication, spontaneity, and lots of laughter do the trick. "Do something out of the ordinary. For a quick getaway go stay at an inn together. It's sometimes nice to wake up in a bed that isn't yours."

Menu

Maine Lobster Salad

Oregon, Müller-Thurgau—Sokol Blosser Winery

Spinach-Stuffed Lamb Chop Pairs

California Zinfandel—Ravenswood Sonoma

Your favorite flourless chocolate cake

Rhode Island Claret—Sakonnet Vineyards

—

Maine Lobster Salad

For the dressing

1 large shallot, finely chopped

1 tablespoon champagne vinegar

3 tablespoons extra virgin olive oil

½ tablespoon sherry wine vinegar

Salt and freshly ground black pepper

For the salad

1 tablespoon extra virgin olive oil

Two 1-ounce slices (½ inch thick) herbed goat cheese

½ cup fine dry bread crumbs

1½ cups baby field greens, washed and spun dry

2 rock lobster tails (6 ounces each), steamed, meat removed, and shells reserved for garnish

10 spears fresh asparagus, peeled, cooked until crunch tender, and cut into 1-inch pieces

1 tablespoon caviar, for garnish

> This salad uses three purportedly romantic ingredients: lobster, asparagus, and cheese. Be sure to follow the directions of the dressing explicitly in order to pull the sensational flavors in this dish together.
> ⎯

1 IN A mixing bowl, whisk together the shallots and the champagne vinegar. Slowly pour in the olive oil, whisking constantly until the mixture is emulsified. Whisk in the sherry vinegar and season to taste with salt and pepper. Set aside.

2 TO PREPARE the salad, preheat the broiler. Line a baking sheet with aluminum foil and brush with oil. Roll the cheese in the bread crumbs, patting the crumbs firmly into the cheese. Set the slices of cheese on the aluminum foil.

3 IN A mixing bowl, toss the salad greens with about 2 tablespoons of the dressing. Place a small mound of greens in the center of a serving plate. Cut the lobster meat into medallions (½-inch slices). In the same mixing bowl, toss the lobster and asparagus pieces with a small quantity of dressing, spoon into the lobster shell, and set it on top of the greens. Or use the shell as decorative garnish, red side up.

4 SET THE cheese under the broiler and broil until it begins to soften and the crumbs are light brown, about 1 minute. Watch carefully so that it doesn't burn. Using a flexible spatula, transfer the warm cheese to the salad. Using a table fork, break up the cheese over the center. Garnish the salad with caviar and serve.

Spinach-Stuffed Lamb Chop Pairs

For the stuffing

One 10-ounce package frozen
    chopped spinach, thawed
1 tablespoon olive oil
1 tablespoon butter
1 shallot, minced
1 small clove garlic, minced
1 ounce chèvre, crumbled
1 tablespoon Parmesan cheese

For the marinade

1 tablespoon balsamic vinegar
1 tablespoon brandy
1 teaspoon Dijon mustard
½ teaspoon fresh rosemary,
    or ¼ teaspoon dried
1 clove garlic, minced

½ teaspoon dried tarragon
½ teaspoon chopped fresh rosemary,
    or ¼ teaspoon dried
½ teaspoon freshly squeezed lemon
    juice
¼ teaspoon salt
¼ teaspoon freshly ground black
    pepper

¼ teaspoon freshly ground black
    pepper
4 well-trimmed 1- to 1½-inch-thick
    loin lamb chops (about 3½ ounces
    each after trimming)
Coarse salt
¼ to ⅓ cup water or broth

1 USING A cotton towel, squeeze all the moisture out of the spinach. Set a large nonstick skillet over medium heat, add the olive oil and butter, and, when the foam subsides, cook the shallot and garlic, stirring, until softened. Stir in the spinach and mix well. Melt in the chèvre. Add the Parmesan cheese, tarragon, rosemary, and lemon juice. The mixture will be rather dry. Off the heat, add the salt and pepper, taste, and correct the seasonings. Cool completely before stuffing the lamb chops.

2 TO MAKE the marinade, whisk together the vinegar, brandy, mustard, rosemary, garlic, and pepper in a small mixing bowl. Place the

At The Putney Inn, Ann stuffs a 6-pound leg of lamb (to serve 8 people) with spinach mixed with chèvre and Parmesan cheese, rosemary, and licorice-flavored tarragon. The rich flavor of this combination marries well with a brandy-marinated lamb. Here we use the stuffing, which may be made ahead, for lamb chops. You will have enough stuffing for 8 to 10 chops, so freeze what you don't use—you never know when he'll beg for lamb chops again!

lamb chops in a flat glass dish, pour the marinade over, cover with plastic wrap, and marinate for 1 hour at room temperature or up to 6 hours in the refrigerator.

3 JUST BEFORE cooking, remove the chops and discard the marinade. Cut a "pocket" in each chop, push about 2 teaspoonfuls of the stuffing into each pocket, and press the edges of the meat together to seal.

4 SET A skillet over high heat, sprinkle a pinch of coarse salt on the pan, and, when the pan is very hot, sear the chops until they are brown, about 3 minutes on each side. Set the chops aside. Add ¼ to ⅓ cup water to the pan, bring to a boil, and cook until the liquid is reduced by half, about 2 minutes. Return the chops to the pan and cook until they are tender or done according to personal preference, 2 to 3 minutes longer, depending on the thickness of the chops. Transfer the chops to warm dinner plates, add a splash of brandy to the skillet, cook the pan juices until they are reduced to a glaze, spoon the glaze over the chops, and serve at once.

TWENTY YEARS AGO when a man wanted to impress a woman he would take her out to a big fancy restaurant. Robert Del Grande took the advice of his grandmother who cooked at home only for "special" people. He invited his crush, Mimi, to his house for dinner. "Back then," he says, "guys didn't cook dinner on a date. But I thought it was a pretty cool way to catch a girl."

As it turned out, cooking dinner was the only way Robert was going to catch Mimi, who had recently moved to Texas. He had just completed his doctorate in biochemistry in California and needed a break. He followed Mimi to Houston, where her sister and brother-in-law owned Café Annie. Robert started working there just to make a little pocket change. It wasn't long before he transformed the kitchen into a culinary science lab—experimenting with Mexican flavors to come up with his version of cowboy cuisine.

Today, Del Grande oversees the kitchen while his wife Mimi manages the restaurant. How does the couple handle working together? Robert sums up their success in two words: "Yes, Ma'am!"

Catching the love of your life is easy with Robert's recipes for romance. Chef Del Grande is "a big fan of simplicity, but simplicity that resonates tremendous power." Instead of smothering your dishes in heavy sauce or extra spices, strive to bring out the essence of just a few ingredients. Also, he says, be careful not to overstuff yourself. "It's a bummer if you have that snake who ate the goat feeling. Go for a walk after dinner."

Why go through all this fuss? Because, once you are married—but before you have children—you won't need to take that much trouble to impress your better half. "Before we had our daughter, we would get take-out, rent three videos, and spend the night eating fried chicken in bed."

Robert Del Grande

Café Annie

Houston, Texas

Menu

Filet Mignon with Avocado and Sea Salt

Cilantro and Serrano Chile Rice

California Chardonnay—Newton Vineyard Napa Valley, 1997

Coffee Ice Cream with Meringues

47

Filet Mignon with Avocado and Sea Salt

1 perfectly ripe Hass avocado
Freshly squeezed lime juice
2 first-quality filet mignon steaks, 6 to
    8 ounces each, 1½ inches thick
1 teaspoon very good coarse sea salt

Freshly ground black pepper
2 tablespoons best-quality extra virgin
    olive oil
A few cilantro sprigs for garnish

1 HALVE, PIT, and peel the avocado. Cut into ¼-inch-thick lengthwise slices and drizzle a splash of lime juice over them.

2 SEASON THE filets mignons with salt and pepper. Lightly flatten each filet with your hand. Set a sauté pan over very high heat, coat the pan with a film of oil, and, when the oil begins to smoke, add the filets and sear them for about 2 minutes on each side, until nicely brown but very rare. Transfer to an ovenproof pan fitted with a roasting rack.

3 PREHEAT THE oven to 350°F. When ready to serve, finish cooking the filets in the oven for 10 to 15 minutes for medium rare or according to personal preference.

4 SERVE THE filets mignons on warm dinner plates. Gently lay a few slices of avocado over each filet, sprinkle with sea salt, and drizzle olive oil over the whole affair. Garnish with cilantro sprigs and serve with Cilantro and Serrano Chile Rice (recipe follows).

Cilantro and Serrano Chile Rice

1¾ cups chicken stock

1 teaspoon salt

1 cup white aromatic rice (preferably
   Texmati brand)

1 tablespoon unsalted butter, softened

Half a medium white onion, minced

1 to 2 serrano chiles, stemmed,
   seeded, and minced

¼ cup minced cilantro leaves

The piquant flavors of cilantro and serrano chile pepper, the staples of cowboy cuisine, dress up the romantic aromatic rice.

1 IN A 1-quart saucepan over high heat, combine the chicken stock, salt, and rice. Bring to a boil, stir well, and cover the pan. Reduce the heat to very low and simmer until all the water is absorbed, about 15 to 18 minutes.

2 COMBINE THE butter, onion, serrano chile, and cilantro in a small bowl. Stir the cilantro mixture into the hot rice until the butter melts and the ingredients are well distributed. Cover the pan and let stand for 5 minutes.

Coffee Ice Cream with Meringues

For a simple way to end the evening, purchase meringues or meringue kisses from your local bakery and serve them with premium coffee ice cream topped with Chocolate Sauce (page 17).

In Colonial Williamsburg, The Trellis Restaurant, surrounded by restored dwellings and charming eighteenth-century decor, survives as a modern-day treasure. Marcel Desaulniers, a.k.a. the Ganache Guru, oversees the delectable creations of his establishment.

Chef Desaulniers teaches his staff how to create memories. "The meal is not something that people can take off the shelf or out of a drawer to look at. It's gone, so the more that we put into the meal, the more the memory will carry." He applies this philosophy to the home-cooked meal as well. "You can get Chinese take-out and have a romantic dinner, but the more personal attention one puts into the meal, the greater the impression. The marvelous thing about cooking for someone is that you are doing something physical. I think that when someone cooks for someone else, he or she knows that tender loving care went into the preparation."

Marcel tried following his own advice when he invited a young woman named Connie to his apartment for dinner. Worried about having enough time for the preparations, he decided to leave dessert in the hands of a friend and highly regarded pastry chef, who baked a delectable baba au rhum. Then he finished cooking too early. "She was due over at seven-thirty, and I called her at a quarter after six and said, 'Dinner's ready now, could you come over sooner?' She found out early on that I was very prompt." Despite the timing, dinner was a success and Connie, who was doubly impressed that he "didn't put the big moves on her that evening," stuck around for many more meals. In fact, they have just celebrated their twenty-second anniversary.

Menu

Wild Mushrooms and Fresh Herbs

California Pinot Noir—Robert Sinskey Los Carneros, 1995

Duck Breast and Shrimp with Broccoli, Country Ham, and Pine-Nut Butter

Rhône Châteauneuf-du-Pape— Domaine de Beaucastel, 1992

Chocolate Rapture

Port—Warre Vintage, 1985

51

Wild Mushrooms and Fresh Herbs

Cooked mushrooms are sensual delicacies. In this first course, wild mushrooms are braised with stock and fresh herbs, then enriched with cream.

—

1 tablespoon olive oil
1 shallot, minced
½ pound wild mushrooms, stemmed
    and sliced ¼ inch thick
Salt and freshly cracked black pepper

⅛ teaspoon chopped fresh dill
⅛ teaspoon chopped fresh tarragon
⅛ teaspoon chopped fresh thyme
1 cup chicken or vegetable stock, hot
¼ cup heavy cream

1 HEAT THE olive oil in a large sauté pan over medium heat. Add the shallot and cook, stirring, for 1 minute. Add the wild mushrooms and season with salt and pepper to taste. Adjust the heat to medium high and cook, stirring, for 2 to 3 minutes. Add the herbs and continue to cook, stirring, until the mushrooms are tender, 3 to 4 minutes.

2 ADD THE stock and bring the mixture to a simmer. Remove from the heat. Add the cream and stir gently to combine. Adjust the seasoning with salt and pepper and serve immediately.

Duck Breast and Shrimp with Broccoli, Country Ham, and Pine-Nut Butter

Two 4-ounce boneless and skinless
    duck breasts
2 tablespoons pine nuts, toasted
    (page 12)
4 tablespoons unsalted butter, softened
Salt and freshly cracked black pepper
1 pound broccoli, stems trimmed, cut
    into florets

½ tablespoon olive oil
¾ pound large shrimp, peeled,
    deveined, and halved lengthwise
⅛ pound country ham or prosciutto,
    cut into strips 1½ inches long and
    ⅛ inch wide

1 TRIM ANY excess fat and membrane from the duck breasts. Place the breasts, one at a time, between two sheets of lightly oiled aluminum foil or parchment paper and flatten them uniformly with a meat cleaver. Cover the duck breasts with plastic wrap and refrigerate until needed.

2 FINELY CHOP all but ½ tablespoon of the nuts. Combine the chopped nuts with the softened butter. Set aside.

3 PREHEAT THE oven to 225°F.

4 LIGHTLY SEASON the duck breasts on both sides with salt and pepper. Heat a dry nonstick sauté pan over high heat. Sear the duck breasts for about 2 minutes on each side, until lightly browned. Remove to a baking sheet and baste each with 1 tablespoon pine-nut butter. Place the duck breasts in the preheated oven for 10 to 12 minutes.

5 COOK THE broccoli florets in boiling salted water until tender but still crunchy, 2½ to 3 minutes. Drain thoroughly. Keep warm until needed.

6 SET A nonstick sauté pan over medium-high heat, add the oil, and, when the oil is hot, add the shrimp and ham, season very lightly with salt and more generously with pepper, and cook, stirring, for 3 to 4 minutes. Remove the pan from the heat. *continued*

Just like lovers, shrimp and duck are opposites that attract. Although this is a simple dish, the complexity of the flavors and textures hasn't been matched since Scarlett first met Rhett. You can substitute chicken breast for the duck; or if your budget—like your passion—knows no limits, use pheasant to win your lover's heart.

7 ALONG THE outer edge of each of two warm 9- or 10-inch soup or pasta plates, arrange the broccoli in a ring, stem ends toward the center. Place a duck breast in the center and spoon the shrimp and ham mixture around each breast. Top with 1 tablespoon of the remaining pine-nut butter, sprinkle the whole pine nuts over the arrangement, and serve.

Chocolate Rapture

8 ounces semisweet chocolate, broken into ½-ounce pieces
¾ cup heavy cream
1 tablespoon unsalted butter
1 tablespoon granulated sugar

¼ cup dark rum
1 pint strawberries with long stems, lightly rinsed and patted dry with paper towels

1 PLACE THE chocolate in a 3-quart bowl.

2 IN A 1½-quart saucepan set over medium-high heat, combine the cream, butter, and sugar. When hot, stir to dissolve the sugar and bring the mixture to a boil. Remove from the heat and immediately pour the hot liquid over the chocolate; allow to stand for 5 minutes. Add the rum and whisk vigorously until smooth. Transfer the rapture to a pretty glass bowl and arrange the berries on a platter.

Love Note: Best served slightly warm, Chocolate Rapture will keep at a perfect dipping temperature for several hours if the bowl is placed on a heating pad set on medium.

Chocolate has long captured the hearts of the amorously inclined and the hedonistically determined.

FRANÇOIS DIONOT WAS once told, "Cooking is the most fun thing to do standing up!" As co-owner of Café Bethesda and director of the Academy of Culinary and Pastry Arts, he must be having a ball. Born in Reims, France, François has spent over thirty years in front of the stove.

When a man loves a woman, he cooks her veal medallions with mushrooms and cream, as François did when he was courting his wife, Patrice. After luring her to his apartment, he seduced Patrice over dinner. The foreplay ended with crème brûlée. "I make lots of crème brûlée," François says. "It's Patrice's favorite. I like foods that have contrasting textures and this is one of the few desserts that has that—a creamy inside and a crisp caramelized shell. When I eat it, I get a lot of pleasure. Combine that with the beautiful woman sitting next to me and my whole body gets excited!"

If cooking is to be a prelude to romance, François urges us to use all five senses. Your guest should "hear singing, the sight should be beautiful, the smell, aromatic, and the touch, soft—of course with permission only." Delicious taste is paramount, and so Dionot recommends your sampling the seductive supper beforehand. "If you don't like what you are eating, you aren't going to put any love into it. After all, the way to a woman's heart is definitely through her stomach!"

Menu

Cold Velouté of Asparagus with Shrimp

White Burgundy—Louis Jadot

Corton-Charlemagne Grand Cru Champagne

Veal Medallions with Mushrooms and Cream

Crème Brûlée

———

Cold Velouté of Asparagus with Shrimp

¾ pound asparagus, peeled
   (see page 11)
1½ tablespoons butter
Half a medium onion, chopped
1 medium leek (white part only),
   trimmed and sliced

Half a large baking potato, peeled and
   cubed
1½ cups chicken stock
Salt and freshly ground pepper
½ to ¾ cup heavy cream
6 medium shrimp, cooked

1 CUT THE tips off 6 asparagus spears and reserve for garnish. Coarsely chop the rest of the asparagus.

2 IN A medium-heavy casserole set over low heat, melt the butter. When the foam subsides, add the onion and leek, cover, and sweat until the vegetables are soft and translucent, about 5 minutes. Raise the heat to medium and add the asparagus, potato, and chicken stock. Season with salt and pepper, bring to a boil, and reduce the heat to a simmer. Cook, uncovered, until the vegetables are soft, about 20 minutes.

3 WORKING IN batches, transfer the mixture to a food processor or blender, process, and pass through a sieve set over a bowl. Cover with plastic wrap and refrigerate for at least 4 hours.

4 COOK THE asparagus tips in boiling salted water for 3 minutes and cool in ice water. Drain well and set aside until serving time.

5 JUST BEFORE serving, whisk the cream into the soup, taste, and correct the seasonings. Ladle the soup into bowls and arrange the shrimp in the center surrounded by asparagus tips.

One of Chef Dionot's favorite recipes, this velvety chilled soup is soft on the tongue. The contrasting textures of crunchy blanched asparagus tips and plump shrimp floating on top are thought to have visually arousing qualities.

—

Veal Medallions with Mushrooms and Cream

12 ounces veal cut for scallopini
Salt and freshly ground black pepper
2 tablespoons peanut or canola oil
2 tablespoons chopped shallots
½ pound button mushrooms, wiped clean and cut into small pieces or slices

¼ cup dry sherry
1½ cups heavy cream
1 tablespoon chopped fresh parsley

1 SLICE THE veal into thin medallions (or have the butcher do this for you), making 6 to 8 thin 3- to 4-inch round slices. Season with salt and pepper.

2 COAT WITH oil the bottom of a heavy skillet; set over high heat, and heat to the smoking point. Quickly sauté the veal for about 2 minutes on both sides. Transfer the meat to a plate and set aside.

3 TO THE same pan over high heat, add the shallots and mushrooms and cook, shaking the pan often, until the mushrooms squeak, about 2 minutes. Add the sherry, deglaze the bottom of the pan, and cook until the liquid is reduced by half, about 3 minutes.

4 ADD THE cream and boil, stirring occasionally, until the sauce thickens, 5 to 6 minutes. Taste and correct the seasonings. Can be done ahead to this point and held for up to 1 hour. (Reheat the sauce before proceeding.)

5 ADD THE meat to the sauce and reheat briefly, about 2 minutes. Do not overcook the meat in the cream sauce.

6 TRANSFER TO a serving plate, sprinkle with parsley, and serve at once with steamed rice.

Love Note: After the veal, serve a salad made with Boston, red-leaf, and romaine lettuces tossed with mustard vinaigrette and tiny cherry tomatoes.

Crème Brûlée

2 large egg yolks

5 tablespoons sugar, divided

½ teaspoon vanilla extract

1 cup heavy cream

1 PREHEAT THE oven to 300°F. Butter the insides of two 6-ounce ramekins. Arrange a water bath: Take a pan large enough to hold the ramekins, half fill it with water, and set it in the oven.

2 WHISK THE egg yolks and gradually add 3 tablespoons of the sugar and the vanilla. Whisk well.

3 SET A small heavy saucepan over high heat, add the cream, and bring to the boiling point. Stirring constantly but gently, pour the hot cream over the egg mixture. Do not create a foam. Strain the mixture into the ramekins, place them in the water bath, and cook until set (a knife inserted into the center comes out clean), 20 to 25 minutes. Do not overcook.

4 CHILL UNTIL ready to serve. Remove from the refrigerator, sprinkle the remaining 2 tablespoons of sugar over the tops, and caramelize with a hot blowtorch. (If you are timid, preheat the broiler to high, set the ramekins 3 inches from the flame under the broiler, and watch carefully until the sugar is caramelized, about 2 minutes.)

A staple in the culinary art of seduction, the silky cream sealed in a sugary shell is Mrs. Dionot's favorite. It must be made a day in advance to allow time for chilling. Use a small blowtorch (available at most housewares stores) to caramelize the top. A broiler works just as well but isn't quite as thrilling to watch.

Jean-Louis Dumonet

Trois Jean

New York

TROIS JEAN, A charming French bistro, nestles among the towering apartment buildings of Manhattan's Upper East Side. Its story is that of three Frenchmen named Jean who made their culinary dreams come true.

The youngest, the executive chef, Jean-Louis Dumonet, put his cooking skills to a severe test seventeen years ago when he proposed to his wife, Karen. Smitten from the very beginning when he met her at the Paris Hotel School, Jean-Louis desperately wanted to impress her when it came time to pop the question. His secret weapon came in the shape of diver scallops, which Karen's mother, a native of Malaysia, used to prepare with blends of spices and curries for her daughter since her childhood. Not yet a master of such ingredients, Jean-Louis chose instead to pan sear the plump delicacies, adding a fresh ginger sauce and mashed new potatoes. Apparently, Karen didn't mind the change; after dinner, she agreed to be his bride.

"Simplicity is the key to good taste," Jean-Louis asserts, advising us not to confuse the diner's palate—a lesson he learned from his grandmother who lived in the Poitou region of France. His advice for blossoming romance is also simple; he likes flowers, but he doesn't like fragrant bouquets. "You can't smell the cooking." He recommends light entrées and, for dessert, "chocolate is always good for romance." Jean-Louis would serve champagne, but if you prefer, "a bottle of white and then a bottle of red—enough wine to enjoy the evening, but not too much or your guest is likely to pass out."

Menu

Soft-Shell Crabs with Pacific Rim Curry Sauce

Mixed Green Salad

Rockfish with Sprouts and Wild Rice

Champagne—Dom Ruinart Blanc de Blancs, 1988

Warm Chocolate Cakes

Soft-Shell Crabs with Pacific Rim Curry Sauce

For the batter

½ cup all-purpose flour

2 egg whites

2 tablespoons cold beer

2 tablespoons water

1 teaspoon curry powder (preferably Madras)

1 teaspoon salt

1 teaspoon freshly ground black pepper

For the sauce

4 tablespoons butter

2 tablespoons curry powder (preferably Madras)

2 tablespoons soy sauce

1 tablespoon grated fresh ginger

1 stalk lemongrass (bottom 3 inches only), minced

2 teaspoons sugar

1 small clove garlic, chopped

1 teaspoon Hunan red chile sauce

1 cup coconut milk

Canola or peanut oil for frying

4 small soft-shell crabs, cleaned, rinsed, and patted dry

Half a medium red bell pepper, julienned

Half a medium tart green apple (Granny Smith), julienned

2 tablespoons chopped cilantro

The combination of crunchy shells, soft insides, and intense flavor makes these crustaceans the perfect starter. The crabs are dipped into a curry-scented beer batter, fried, and then presented with a spicy Pacific Rim sauce that is accented with apple, sweet bell pepper, and spicy cilantro.

1 PREPARE THE batter in a food processor. Process the flour, ¼ cup egg white (measure out and discard any leftovers), beer, water, curry powder, salt, and pepper until smooth and well blended, about 3 minutes. Transfer to a shallow bowl.

2 TO MAKE the sauce, set a small nonreactive saucepan over medium heat, melt the butter, and cook the curry powder, stirring, until aromatic, about 1 minute. Add the soy sauce, ginger, lemongrass, sugar, garlic, and chile sauce, and bring to a boil. Add the coconut milk and continue cooking for about 5 minutes. Strain the sauce into a clean saucepan and keep warm.

3 INTO A skillet set over high heat, pour about 1 inch of canola or peanut oil. When the oil shimmers, dip the crabs into the batter and shake off the excess. Fry the crabs in the hot oil until golden brown on both sides, 2 to 3 minutes on each side. Transfer to a plate lined with paper towels.

4 STIR THE bell pepper and apple into the hot sauce, taste, and correct the seasonings. Ladle enough of the sauce to cover the center of the heated plates, place the crabs on the sauce, sprinkle cilantro over the whole affair, and serve at once.

Rockfish with Sprouts and Wild Rice

¼ cup wild rice

Sea salt and freshly ground black pepper

½ cup good-quality fish stock or bottled clam juice

¼ cup dry vermouth

2 tablespoons soy sauce

6 tablespoons unsalted butter, divided

½ cup fresh bean sprouts, rinsed and patted dry

6 sprigs fresh cilantro, chopped

1 medium firm, ripe tomato, peeled, seeded, and diced

1 teaspoon five-spice powder

Two 6-ounce fillets rockfish (or red snapper or striped bass), with skin on

1 ONE DAY AHEAD, place the wild rice in a small bowl with enough cold water to cover it by 1 inch and soak it overnight. The next day, drain the rice and rinse it with fresh cold water. Transfer the rice to a medium saucepan set over high heat, add enough fresh water to cover by 1 inch, and bring to a boil. Cook until the rice is tender, about 20 minutes. Season with salt and pepper and set aside.

2 MEANWHILE, IN a medium saucepan over high heat, bring the fish stock and vermouth to a boil and cook until the liquid is reduced to ¼ cup. Remove from the heat, add the soy sauce, swirl 2 tablespoons of the butter into the reduction, and reserve.

3 IN A small sauté pan set over high heat, melt 2 tablespoons of butter. When the foam subsides, add the wild rice and bean sprouts and cook, stirring, until the sprouts are heated through, about 3 minutes. Add the cilantro, tomato, and five-spice powder, mix well, taste, and correct the seasonings.

4 IN A small skillet over high heat, melt the remaining butter. Sear the fish, when the foam subsides, skin side down first, until brown on both sides and the flesh looks opaque, 5 to 6 minutes total cooking time.

5 MOUND A large scoop of the rice and sprout mixture in the center of warm dinner plates, pour some sauce around, and place the fish on top.

The mild and sweet flavor of the firm Pacific Coast fish is the perfect underpinning for an entrée that includes earthy and rich wild rice (which needs to be soaked overnight) and mild and crunchy bean sprouts. Topped with a hint of cilantro, this sultry fish is encircled with a soy-infused buttery sauce—utterly delicious.

Warm Chocolate Cakes

2 ounces Valrhona bittersweet
    chocolate, cut into ¼-inch pieces
3 tablespoons unsalted butter
1 large egg
1 large egg yolk

4½ tablespoons sugar
2 tablespoons plus 2 teaspoons flour
5 aluminum foil cupcake cases
    (the 4-ounce size is best), buttered
    and floured

1 PREHEAT THE oven to 400°F. Set a rack in the middle of the oven.

2 FILL A saucepan with water, bring to a boil, and turn off the heat. In a metal mixing bowl, combine the chocolate and butter and place it over the water. Stir occasionally until melted, about 8 minutes. Set the bowl aside to cool slightly.

3 IN A mixing bowl, beat the egg and egg yolk together until frothy. Gradually add the sugar, and then the chocolate and butter mixture. Fold in the flour gently. Fill the foil cases, leaving only ¼ inch at the top. (Cover with plastic wrap and refrigerate for up to 5 hours, if necessary.)

4 BAKE ON the center rack of the oven for 8 to 10 minutes. Unmold one (this is the test cake) to see how liquid it is; the cake should be firm enough to hold its shape but still be soft and runny in the center. Touch the top with your finger lightly—it should jiggle a bit.

5 UNMOLD THE remaining cakes onto warm plates, top with a scoop of vanilla ice cream, and serve at once.

"THE REASON I started cooking was a woman," says Rocky Durham, co-executive chef of Santacafe in Santa Fe, New Mexico. "I was thirteen years old and had a huge crush on this older woman who worked as a baker." (She was fifteen.) "I got a job as a dishwasher in the restaurant just so that I could be close to her. The chef saw what was happening—how I couldn't take my eyes off her—so he moved me into the kitchen. The romance went nowhere, but it did launch my career in cooking."

His partner, David Sellers, waited until he was a bit older and more experienced in the kitchen to impress a girl. "I cooked my girlfriend a three-course meal, goat cheese soufflé, pasta with lobster and asparagus, and a peach tartlet with crème fraîche. We moved in together almost immediately after that!"

For the past three years, the pair has been filling the hearts and stomachs of the guests at the Santacafe, showing off such Southwestern delights as shiitake and cactus spring rolls with green chile dipping salsa and grilled free-range New Mexican chicken breast with crabapple compote and green chile mashed potatoes. Aside from the food, diners can experience the real flavors of Santa Fe just by sitting in the courtyard of the historic adobe among the locust and apricot trees under a starlit periwinkle sky.

Despite long hours at the restaurant, these men in aprons still like cooking at home. "Chicks dig it," Rocky jokes. "But, seriously, when I cook for a woman, there is something very powerful involved. It's something that I don't take for granted, mostly because I can't get off work unless it's for a special occasion."

To serve this glorious meal at home, David thinks that there are two roads to take. "You can set up an elegant dining room and serve the food plate by plate or you can eat the first course standing up and hang out in the kitchen while you work on the other courses."

Rocky Durham
and
David Sellers

Santacafe

Santa Fe, New Mexico

Menu

Chilled Lime Shrimp Salad

Slow-Roasted Salmon with Spring Vegetable Ragout

Sauvignon Blanc

Strawberry *Clafoutis*

65

Chilled Lime Shrimp Salad

The beauty of this prelude is that the preparatory work is done behind the scenes, long before your lover sees it. Arrange all the ingredients, and, at the appropriate moment, uncork the wine and nibble on these zesty flavored shrimp served with avocado and a lime-scented crème fraîche.

1 bunch cilantro, chopped

1 serrano chile, seeded and minced

2 cloves garlic, minced

2 limes, zested and juiced, plus juice of 1 lime (reserve 1 teaspoon of juice for the crème fraîche)

½ cup canola oil

12 large shrimp, peeled and deveined

Salt and freshly ground black pepper

1 firm, ripe Hass avocado, sliced lengthwise and tossed gently, in lime juice

1 tomato, diced

3 ounces crème fraîche

2 tablespoons chopped chives

1 WHISK THE cilantro, chile, garlic, lime zest, and juice together with the canola oil. Add the shrimp to the mixture and marinate for half an hour in the refrigerator.

2 POUR OFF the marinade. Set a sauté pan over high heat, add the shrimp, sprinkle with salt and pepper, and cook until the shrimp begin to color on the first side, about 2 minutes. Turn the shrimp over and cook until they turn opaque, about 1 minute longer. Immediately remove from the pan and place on a plate. Cover with plastic wrap and refrigerate.

3 ON A serving plate, arrange the avocado slices in spoke fashion and scatter the diced tomato over the avocado. Place the chilled shrimp on top.

4 WHISK THE crème fraîche with the reserved teaspoon of lime juice. Put a dollop on the side of the serving plate and top the shrimp with chives.

Slow-Roasted Salmon with Spring Vegetable Ragout

For the marinade
⅓ cup canola oil
½ tablespoon light brown sugar
1 tablespoon pure red chile powder
  (preferably Chimayo)
1 teaspoon each ground cumin and
  whole coriander seeds, toasted
  (page 12)

Pinch of salt and freshly ground
  pepper
Two salmon fillets, 6 to 7 ounces each

½ cup fresh fava beans
2 tablespoons butter
4 ounces mixed fresh morels, shiitake,
  and portobello mushrooms, sliced
1 cup fresh baby spinach leaves,
  washed
2 plum tomatoes, seeded and chopped

½ tablespoon fresh basil cut into a chif-
  fonade (reserve a few for garnish)
¾ teaspoon fresh thyme leaves
⅓ cup white wine
2 cups vegetable stock
Salt and freshly ground pepper

> Slow roasting renders marinated salmon irresistibly tender and tasty. The dramatic presentation, sitting atop a ragout of morels, fava beans, and baby spinach in an aromatic broth, is surely a prelude for romance.

1 TO MAKE the marinade, whisk the oil with the sugar, chile powder, cumin, coriander, and salt and pepper. Add the salmon, cover with plastic wrap, and refrigerate for at least 30 minutes or up to 3 hours.

2 DROP THE fava beans into boiling water for 1 minute, then into ice water. When cool, peel, remove the inner skin, and blanch for 5 minutes.

3 PREHEAT THE oven to 250°F. Remove the salmon fillets from the marinade and place them in a roasting pan, skin side down. Roast until the flesh springs back slightly when touched, about 25 minutes for medium rare. Discard the marinade.   *continued*

4 MEANWHILE, MELT the butter in a large nonreactive sauté pan set over high heat. When the foam subsides, cook the mushrooms, shaking the pan, for 3 to 4 minutes. Stir in the fava beans, spinach, tomatoes, basil, and thyme and cook, stirring, for 2 to 3 minutes. Add the wine and reduce to a glaze, about 3 minutes. Taste and correct the seasonings. Add the stock and simmer until the vegetables are tender, about 10 minutes. Add salt and pepper to taste.

5 LADLE THE vegetables with their juices into deep serving bowls or plates. Remove the salmon from the oven and place one fillet on top of the vegetables. Scatter a few slivers of basil on top and serve at once.

Strawberry *Clafoutis*

A new twist on a traditional French country dessert usually made with cherries, this *clafoutis* is made with fresh strawberries cooked on top of the batter and served hot.

2 tablespoons unsalted butter

12 strawberries, washed, drained, and hulled

¾ cup plus 2 tablespoons sugar, divided

1 teaspoon fresh lemon juice

¼ cup walnut or corn oil

2 large eggs

½ teaspoon vanilla extract

1 cup cake flour

Pinch of salt

½ teaspoon baking powder

2 tablespoons powdered sugar

¼ cup fresh orange juice

½ cup heavy cream

1 PREHEAT THE oven to 375°F. Have ready an 8-inch nonstick frying pan and an oiled glass pie plate or oven-to-table gratin dish.

2 IN A sauté pan over medium heat, melt the butter until it just turns golden and the foam subsides. Add the strawberries and cook gently, shaking the pan to stir them. When the berries begin to release their juices, add

½ cup of the sugar and the lemon juice and continue cooking until a buttery caramel forms to coat the berries, about 5 minutes. The strawberries will continue to release their juices, but not collapse completely. When they begin to lose their shape, lift the berries out with a slotted spoon and set aside. Keep the pan juices for the glaze.

3 TO MAKE the batter, mix the oil, eggs, and vanilla together. Sift the flour into the bowl and add the salt, baking powder, and ¼ cup of the remaining sugar. Beat together until smooth.

4 POUR THE batter into the pie plate or gratin dish. Carefully drop the strawberries into the dish one by one, making sure they are evenly scattered through the batter. Dust with the remaining 2 tablespoons sugar and bake until puffed and golden brown, about 25 minutes. Remove from the oven and dust with powdered sugar. (This can be done ahead and the *clafoutis* reheated in the dish, covered with foil, for approximately 12 minutes in a 350°F oven.)

5 JUST BEFORE serving, reheat the pan juices with the orange juice and pour the mixture over the dessert as a glaze. Whip the cream (see page 14), garnish the *clafoutis,* and serve at once.

EIGHT YEARS AGO, Terrance Feury was an up-and-coming chef, putting in long, long hours to make his way to the top of the food chain. So it was a treat when he took time away from the burners to take his high-school sweetheart and now wife, Tara, out to a "real" dinner for St. Valentine's Day. "I ordered salmon. It still reminds me of Valentine's Day; maybe it's the rosy color."

At Striped Bass in Philadelphia, Feury, the executive chef, has made quite a splash. "Cooking with seafood is my passion," he says. Patrons love to view his team preparing all sorts of deep-sea dishes in the open kitchen underneath an enormous metal sculpture of a leaping striped bass.

To keep him from sinking, Tara cooks Terrance breakfast every morning before he heads to the "office." Sometimes she'll surprise him with heart-shaped French toast. Terrance, who is in charge of special dinners, returns the favor with lobster and risotto, salmon (of course), and a dessert of mixed berries and cream. "The risotto is an extravagant dish but easy to make . . . so you can impress someone. And the color of the red wine is sexy to me."

Okay, Romeo, now it's time to let your inner chef shine! Terrance urges not to get too hung up on creating a five-star dinner. "She'll be more impressed with the effort than with every little thing being perfect," he says. So take your time. "You don't want to be wiped out by the time your date arrives." These suggestions worked for a good friend of the chef's who was trying to impress a girlfriend. "I guess it was successful," says Terrance, "because the next day he called me to say, 'I owe you one.' "

Menu

Lobster with Red Wine Risotto

France Côtes-du-Rhône, Rosé—M. Chapoutier, Belleruche, 1995

Pan-Seared Salmon with Black Truffle and Baby Artichokes

Burgundy Pinot Noir—Volnay, Domaine de Montille, Taillepieds, 1992

Mixed Berries with Whipped Cream

Piedmont, Italy—Moscato d'Asti, Bera, 1997

Lobster with Red Wine Risotto

For the risotto

1 cup dry red wine

¼ cup port

¼ cup unsalted butter

1 shallot, finely minced

½ cup Arborio rice

1 cup chicken stock, boiling

¼ cup freshly grated Parmesan cheese

For the sauce

1 cup chicken stock, boiling

¼ cup extra virgin olive oil

½ cup freshly grated Parmesan cheese

Ground white pepper

1 tablespoon butter

Two 1- to 1¼-pound Maine lobsters, steamed, shells removed, tail split, and meat cut into bite-size pieces

Shaved Parmesan, for garnish

2 sprigs chervil, for garnish

> The natural sweetness of the lobster and the saltiness of the risotto blend to create a beautifully balanced starter for a romantic evening.

1 IN A nonreactive saucepan set over high heat, bring the red wine and port to a boil, reduce the heat, and simmer until reduced by half, about 5 minutes.

2 SET A heavy saucepan over medium heat, add the butter, and cook the shallot, stirring, for 2 minutes. Add the rice and cook, stirring, for 2 minutes. Add the reduced wine and simmer until all the liquid is absorbed. Gently stirring while cooking, add about ¼ cup of the chicken stock at a time, cooking until all the liquid is absorbed before adding more. Cook until the rice is *al dente*. Stir in the Parmesan cheese.

3 TO MAKE the sauce, pour the hot stock into a blender and start blending on low then gradually increase the speed to high. Slowly add the olive oil through the feeding tube; the sauce will look white and creamy. Add the cheese and mix just until blended. Season to taste with pepper. If the sauce is too thick, add a little more hot chicken stock.

continued

4 To finish the dish, melt the butter in a small saucepan over medium heat and add the lobster meat and about 2 tablespoons water. Cook just until the lobster meat is warm, 2 to 3 minutes.

5 Serve this in warmed large, flat soup bowls. Place a mound of the risotto in the center, spoon a little of the creamy sauce around the risotto, place the lobster on top, and garnish with shaved Parmesan and a sprig of chervil.

Pan-Seared Salmon with Black Truffle and Baby Artichokes

1 cup small fingerling potatoes (or substitute new red potatoes)

½ cup diced celery root

½ cup unsalted butter at room temperature

1 fresh black truffle, finely chopped

1 tablespoon extra virgin olive oil

4 baby artichokes, cooked and quartered

2 tablespoons snipped chives, for garnish

Coarse salt and freshly ground black pepper

Two 6-ounce salmon fillets, with skin

¼ cup chicken stock, hot

> This is a dish to soften the heart of the most hardened meat-and-potatoes person. The salmon cooks in less than five minutes, so have all the vegetables cooked ahead of time.

1 IN A medium saucepan set over high heat, bring 2 to 3 cups of water to a boil, add a pinch of salt, and cook the potatoes until tender, about 10 minutes; drain and set aside. In another saucepan set over high heat, bring 2 cups of salted water to a boil and cook the celery root until tender, about 5 minutes; drain and set aside.

2 USING A food processor, mix the butter and truffle until smooth.

3 HEAT THE olive oil in a sauté pan set over medium heat, and fry the potatoes, celery root, and artichokes, stirring, until the vegetables are light brown on the edges, about 3 minutes. Add half of the chives and season to taste with salt and pepper. Place the vegetables onto two warm dinner plates.

4 SEASON THE salmon fillets with salt and pepper. Heat a sauté pan over high heat until it is nearly smoking, sprinkle the pan with a pinch of coarse salt, and sear the salmon, skin-side down, until the skin is brown, 2 to 3 minutes. Sear the other side, 2 to 3 minutes, for medium rare. The cooking time depends on the thickness of the fish. Set the fish on top of the vegetables.

5 DISCARD ANY fat left in the sauté pan, set the pan back over high heat, add the chicken stock, and bring to a boil. Reduce the heat and slowly whisk in the truffle butter. Remove from the heat and spoon the truffle sauce around the salmon. Sprinkle with the remaining chives and serve.

Bobby Flay

Bolo and Mesa Grill

New York

WHEN BOBBY FLAY invites a date to his home, she may expect a grand affair and hope that he'll work his freckles off to dazzle her with the talents that have made his restaurants, Bolo and Mesa Grill, famous. This - won't happen. "I don't need to bring someone to my house to prove that I can cook my ass off," Flay says.

When Bobby invites a woman to his home (typically on a second date), he likes keeping things casual. A typical meal might be a steak or a piece of fish served with vegetables roasted in the oven. "*Maybe* I'll throw on some chopped parsley to add color, but that's it!" Despite this approach, Flay has been known to succumb to the oldest trick in the book (certainly it is in this book) and serve caviar. He pauses for a moment and asks, "Has every chef mentioned caviar already?"

Chefs have a technical advantage when it comes to home-cooked meals, but that doesn't mean that they don't get the jitters. "Sometimes, I'll go to the market. Then I'll start to panic because it will be an hour before my date is coming over and I'll still be there!" Bobby prefers to plan ahead. "You can't just worry about the food. You've got to think about cleaning your house and making sure that bathroom sparkles. You also have to think about what could possibly happen after dinner. I mean, what if she spends the night?" His solution is to cover all of the breakfast bases. "I don't know if most guys do this, but I buy Sweet 'N' Low, sugar, orange juice, regular milk, and skim milk."

He loves women who eat steaks, so the I'll-just-have-salad routine is not likely to impress him. "I get disappointed when my date says she's not hungry. I think, Wait a minute, I spent the whole day shopping! Then I *know* I'm stuck with all that milk!"

$\mathcal{M}$enu

Frisée Salad with Chorizo and Balsamic Vinaigrette

Light Côte-du-Rhône

Pan-Grilled Salmon with Yellow Pepper and Saffron Sauce

Pinot Blanc—French or California

Israeli Couscous with Roasted Root Vegetables

Crème Brûlée (Bobby's suggestion for dessert)

Frisée Salad with Chorizo and Balsamic Vinaigrette

For the dressing

2 tablespoons balsamic vinegar

1 large clove garlic, peeled

1½ teaspoons Dijon mustard

2 pinches salt

¼ teaspoon freshly ground black
  pepper

¼ to ⅓ cup olive oil

¼ pound Spanish chorizo sausage,
  sliced ⅛ inch thin

2 cups frisée, washed and torn into
  bite-size pieces

1 medium firm, ripe tomato, cut into
  eighths

¼ pound *Manchego* cheese, finely
  shaved

2 tablespoons chopped fresh cilantro

1 COMBINE THE vinegar, garlic, mustard, salt, and pepper in the bowl of a food processor or blender and process until smooth. Slowly add the olive oil through the feeding tube until the mixture is emulsified. Transfer to a bowl, taste, and correct the seasonings. Cover and store in the refrigerator for up to 2 weeks.

2 IN A sauté pan over medium-high heat, cook the chorizo until golden brown on both sides, 8 to 10 minutes. Drain on paper towels.

3 TOSS THE frisée with 2 to 3 tablespoons of the dressing and divide between 2 dinner plates. Dress the tomatoes with 1 tablespoon of the dressing and arrange on the frisée. Arrange the chorizo, cheese, and cilantro on the top and around the edges of the salad. Drizzle on a bit more dressing and serve.

Frisée is feathery, almost spiky, lettuce. Its mildly bitter flavor and firm texture stand up to the spicy Spanish chorizo sausage and robust taste of this balsamic vinaigrette. If frisée is not available, use a curly chicory that is torn into bite-size pieces. *Manchego* is a semifirm, rich, sheep's-milk Spanish cheese that perfectly marries the greens and sausage in the salad together.

Pan-Grilled Salmon with Yellow Pepper and Saffron Sauce

Yellow peppers and saffron add a glorious brilliant color to the plate when drizzled over the rich salmon. For the best flavor, roast the pepper and toast the saffron. Make the sauce and the couscous with vegetables before the object of your affection arrives. Then all you need to do for the dinner is to grill the salmon.

For the sauce

1 large yellow bell pepper, roasted (page 12) and chopped
3 tablespoons rice vinegar
3 large cloves garlic, chopped
Pinch saffron threads, toasted in a dry skillet over high heat for 1 minute

1½ teaspoons honey
½ teaspoon Dijon mustard
Scant ⅔ cup extra virgin olive oil
Coarse salt and freshly ground black pepper

Two 6-ounce salmon fillets, with skin
1 tablespoon olive oil
Ancho chile powder
Quarter of a large yellow bell pepper, minced, for garnish

Quarter of a large red bell pepper, minced, for garnish

1 IN A blender or food processor, combine the roasted pepper, vinegar, garlic, saffron, honey, and mustard. Blend for 30 seconds. Slowly add the oil through the feeding tube until the sauce emulsifies. Transfer to a bowl and season to taste with salt and pepper. Cover and set aside.

2 PLACE A grill pan over high heat until smoking. Brush the salmon on both sides with olive oil and sprinkle with salt and chile powder to taste. Grill, skin-side down, until golden brown, 2 to 3 minutes. Turn over, lower the heat to medium, and cook 2 to 3 minutes more. Transfer the salmon to a warm dinner plate and drizzle on the sauce. Garnish with finely chopped red and yellow peppers. Serve at once with Israeli Couscous with Roasted Vegetables (recipe follows).

Israeli Couscous
with Roasted Root Vegetables

1 medium carrot, peeled and cut into
   ½-inch cubes

1 medium parsnip, peeled and cut
   into ½-inch cubes

1 medium beet, peeled and cut into
   ½-inch cubes

¼ cup olive oil

Salt and freshly ground black pepper

Half a small red onion, minced

1 large clove garlic, minced

6 ounces Israeli couscous

2 tablespoons red wine vinegar

½ tablespoon puréed canned *chipotle*
   pepper in adobo, or 1 teaspoon
   crushed red pepper flakes

1½ tablespoons minced fresh
   rosemary, or 2 teaspoons dried

2 sage leaves, julienned

½ tablespoon minced fresh thyme, or
   2 teaspoons dried

1½ tablespoons minced cilantro

1 PREHEAT THE oven to 425°F. Line a jelly-roll pan with aluminum foil and lightly film the bottom with oil. Scatter the carrots, parsnips, and beets in the pan, drizzle with enough oil to coat lightly, toss, and season with salt and pepper. Roast until the vegetables are just cooked through, about 25 minutes. Set aside.

2 WARM 1 tablespoon of oil in a medium saucepan set over medium-high heat. Add the onion and cook, stirring, until soft and translucent, about 3 minutes. Add the garlic and cook for 1 minute. Stir in the couscous, adding oil as necessary to coat. Add enough cold water just to cover the couscous. Bring to a boil, cover, reduce the heat, and, following directions on the package, cook until all the water is absorbed. Let cool.

3 ADD THE roasted vegetables to the couscous along with their juices and toss. Add the vinegar, 1 tablespoon of oil, the *chipotle* pepper, rosemary, sage, thyme, and cilantro and toss. Season to taste and serve hot or at room temperature.

Roasting root vegetables deepens their flavor to a mellow sweetness. It's the secret that turns this oversize Middle Eastern couscous into a rich dish that you can serve as a main course. P.S.: Supermarket couscous works just fine as a substitute for Israeli couscous, but the texture will be different.

Diane Forley

Verbena

New York

IF YOU STAY in Manhattan for any length of time, the blaring horns, exhaust fumes, and shoving crowds will eventually seep into your skin. But walking into Verbena, a tranquil nest in Gramercy Park, is like walking into a botanical fairy tale—glass panels embedded with plants and herbs, an earth-toned room drenched in textured fabrics and golden light, and a mystical courtyard garden.

Floating around the dining room, Diane Forley, the executive chef, often surprises her guests by her youth and intriguing beauty. She nourishes her admirers with delights from the Mediterranean and South America, which is where lemon-scented verbena—a herb known for its meditative and sensual qualities—grows wild.

Exactly what is it about this enchanted eatery that creates such an aura of passion? "I think that it's all of the elements," Forley says. "You can't just serve a dish and expect that to work on its own. It takes the setting, the lighting, the music, the fabrics, the food, and the wine." To create such natural splendor at home, Diane recommends a beautiful table display. "I think that the table setting is very important." She would adorn the table with a beautiful cloth, flowers, candles, and even fruits and vegetables.

Believing that how you feel when you eat is as important as how you feel after you eat, Diane advises to avoid spicy or obtrusive ingredients. "When you are trying to be romantic, you don't want to eat something that is going to make you sweat or get stuck in your teeth." She giggles.

Menu

Mixed Greens Salad

Roast Quail with Celery Root,
Leeks, and Quince Chutney

Sauvignon Blanc

Gianduja Pots de Crème

——

Roast Quail with Celery Root, Leeks, and Quince Chutney

For the marinade

2 limes, zested (reserve the limes)

½ teaspoon coarsely ground
    peppercorns

¾ cup olive oil

2 boneless quail (center breast bone
    removed), washed and patted dry

2 large shallots, peeled and thinly
    sliced

8 or 10 whole sprigs fresh thyme

¼ cup plus 1½ tablespoons olive oil

2 leeks (white part only), cleaned
    thoroughly and cut into ¼-inch
    crosswise slices

Salt and freshly ground black pepper

2½ cups chicken stock, divided

1 bunch flat-leaf (Italian) parsley,
    washed and tied with string

1 knob celery root, 3 to 4 inches in
    diameter, peeled and cut into
    1-inch cubes

2 tablespoons store-bought quince
    chutney

1 cup heavy cream

About ⅓ cup brewed chamomile tea

About 2 tablespoons unsalted butter,
    soft

Fresh thyme sprigs, for garnish

1 MARINATE THE quail one day ahead. Mix together the lime zest, peppercorns, and olive oil. Place the quail marinade, shallots, and thyme in a Ziploc bag and refrigerate overnight.

2 PREHEAT THE oven to 450°F. Pour ¼ cup of the olive oil into a large heavy casserole set over high heat. Add the leeks, season with salt and pepper, and sear them, shaking the pan constantly, until light brown, about

A fitting dish to serve your lover, tender quail is best eaten with your fingers. (Chicken breasts or rock Cornish game hens are delicious alternatives.) Marinating the quail not only imparts a foresty flavor to the meat but also tenderizes it. The birds are served on a subtle purée of celery root that is surrounded by leeks and accompanied by a chamomile-flavored quince chutney. Start this recipe one day ahead.

3 minutes. Add 2 cups of the chicken stock and the entire bunch of parsley. Cover and cook in the oven until the leeks are soft and tender, about 10 minutes. Remove from the oven and cool. Discard the parsley, cover the leeks, and refrigerate.

3 TO PREPARE the purée, place the celery root cubes into a medium saucepan set over high heat, cover with cold water, add a pinch or two of salt, and bring to a boil. Cook until soft, about 35 minutes. Drain well. Working in batches, purée the celery root in a food processor. Gradually add about ¼ cup of heavy cream to each batch. Pass the purée through a fine strainer set over a bowl. Taste and correct the seasoning with salt and pepper. Set aside or cover with plastic wrap and refrigerate overnight. Reheat before serving.

4 TO COOK the quail, preheat the oven to 450°F. Remove the birds from the marinade and season them with salt. Discard the marinade. Coat the bottom of a large, heavy, deep casserole with oil and set over high heat. Sear the quail until brown on both sides, about 8 minutes total. Squeeze the reserved limes and pour the juice over the quail. Add ¼ cup of the chicken stock, cover, and roast the birds in the oven until they are tender, about 10 minutes. When done, remove from the pan and set aside in a warm place for 5 minutes.

5 TO MAKE the sauce, set the pan over high heat and deglaze it with the remaining ¼ cup of chicken stock. Stir in the chutney and chamomile tea and mix well. Swirl the butter into the sauce to finish it. Taste and correct the seasoning.

6 TO SERVE, reheat the leeks and the celery root purée until hot. Spoon a serving of purée into the center of a warm plate, surround the purée with leeks, place the quail on top, garnish with fresh thyme, and serve.

Gianduja Pots de Crème

½ cup milk

3 ounces semisweet chocolate, gianduja, or hazelnut milk chocolate, chopped

¾ cup plus 1½ tablespoons heavy cream

3 large egg yolks

⅓ cup plus 1 tablespoon sugar

1 PREHEAT THE oven to 300°F. Half fill a shallow baking pan with water and set in the oven. Butter the insides of three 4-ounce *pots de crème* or ramekins.

2 POUR THE milk into a heavy quart saucepan set over low heat and heat until barely simmering. Stir in the chocolate and remove from the heat. In a mixing bowl, beat the egg yolks until frothy, slowly add the sugar, and whisk until the mixture is light. Slowly pour the hot chocolate mixture into the yolks, whisking constantly. Whisk in the cream. Strain the custard through a fine-mesh strainer set over a metal bowl. Set the bowl in an ice bath for 5 to 10 minutes to chill the custard and keep it creamy.

3 POUR THE custard into *pots de crème* or ramekins. Set the molds in the heated water bath and cover the entire pan with aluminum foil. Bake until the custards are set, about 30 minutes. Refrigerate until cold before serving.

Rich, creamy gianduja or hazelnut milk chocolate gives this dessert its distinctive taste. If hazelnut milk chocolate is unavailable, your favorite variety will work just as well. After sampling this divinely creamy custard, there's a good chance that you'll decide to skip the rest of the meal and go straight for dessert!

Jimmy Gherardi

J's Fresh Seafood
Restaurant

Cincinnati, Ohio

"SHE FILLS THE dishwasher and I empty it." That's the secret to a good marriage, according to Cincinnati's top chef, Jimmy Gherardi, who has been joined in holy matrimony to his wife and "best friend" Susie since 1975. Between running his restaurants, hosting his own radio show, writing cookbooks, and raising a family, Jimmy and his wife find little time for romance. So when his wife wanted to see *Titanic*, instead of waiting through the three-hour movie to eat dinner, he prepared a gourmet picnic.

As a kid, Gherardi was always being shipped off to the movies (the only place in town with air conditioning) with a brown-bagged lunch. "My mother would send us to triple features with veal cutlets in case we got hungry," he remembers.

He surprised his wife by smuggling in a prosciutto and Fontina cheese hero wrapped in a linen napkin, a container of soba noodles with lotus root, a bottle of champagne, and two plastic cups. A nearby viewer, annoyed by all the munching and crunching, was easily bribed with his own cup of champagne.

Besides Susie, the passion in Jimmy's life comes from his love affair with food. He talks about it on the radio. He lives next to his flagship restaurant, J's Fresh Seafood, where his children help out in the kitchen. (His daughter Anna, barely old enough to vote, is already one of Cincinnati's hottest chefs.) He loves giving it as gifts. "I have forty-pound wheels of Locatelli romano cheese. I love cutting off wedges and giving them out to friends . . . if you are in the food business you tend to be a giving person."

Menu

Jimmy's Movie Hero

Champagne—Moët & Chandon

Raisinettes, Goobers, Twizzlers

Jimmy's Movie Hero

For the pesto

3 large cloves garlic, minced

¼ cup minced fresh ginger

½ cup whole scallions, trimmed and
chopped

½ cup chopped fresh basil leaves

¼ cup chopped macadamia nuts

¼ teaspoon ground white pepper

2 teaspoons grated Parmesan cheese

½ cup olive oil

For the sandwich

1 Italian or French baguette

3 ounces prosciutto, sliced paper thin

2 ounces imported provolone or
Fontina cheese, sliced very thin

3 or 4 slices roasted red bell pepper
(page 12) (optional)

1 tomato, thinly sliced (optional)

3 or 4 thin slices red onion (optional)

> Let your imagination run wild when you choose the meat, cheese, and vegetables to stuff inside this warm hero sandwich. Be sure to pair succulent with savory when you let your heart's desire dictate what goes into this meal; you won't even care what movie you see.

1 TO MAKE the pesto, mix the garlic, ginger, scallions, basil, nuts, pepper, and Parmesan cheese in a food processor. Add the olive oil through the feeding tube and process until the mixture forms a paste. Transfer to a container and refrigerate for up to 2 weeks, or until needed.

2 TO MAKE the sandwich, preheat the oven to 350°F. Slice the bread in half lengthwise, discard a bit of the soft white center, and slather about 1 tablespoon of the pesto on each of the top and bottom slices. Place the prosciutto on the bottom half, top with cheese, and add the roasted pepper, tomato, and onion, if using. Cover with the top piece of bread and cut the loaf in half. Wrap each half loaf securely in aluminum foil.

3 BAKE UNTIL the sandwich is heated through, 10 to 15 minutes. Wrap the sandwiches in a pretty cloth napkin to keep warm for the show.

Rozanne Gold

Joseph Baum & Michael
Whiteman Company

Best known for creating
Rainbow Room and
Windows on the World

New York

THE GATES HAVE closed on one of the most romantic restaurants in the world, sixty-five floors high above Manhattan's busy streets, where friends and lovers were whisked back to Fred and Ginger time. Under a stream of shimmering lights, couples twirled around the revolving dance floor. Opened in 1934, the club was once the epicenter of romance.

Rozanne Gold and her husband, Michael Whiteman, once reigned as king and queen of the Rainbow Room. Gold met the love of her life when, despite Whiteman's initial objections, his partner Joe Baum hired her to be the chef director at their restaurant consulting company. "I got even," he says "and married her."

"Michael and I," says Gold, "have two consuming passions: food and each other or, sometimes, the other way around. Together we helped create two of America's most glamorous restaurants: Windows on the World and the magical Rainbow Room. Let me tell you how seductive it really is: We were laboring to rebuild it in 1987 when, perhaps overcome by the heavenly views, Michael asked me to marry him. So ours was the very first wedding. We tripped the light fantastic on the slowly revolving dance floor (that hadn't budged for the previous twenty years) to the beat of a twenty-piece orchestra. Amidst a thousand champagne-colored roses, we fed each other slices of wedding cake and drank Veuve Clicquot. We gazed into each other's eyes, knowing full well what we really wanted. Hearts pounding and hopelessly in love, we slipped into the chef's office and . . . ate a plate of pickled herring!"

Love Note: Order the French Kisses from D'Artagnan, Newark, NJ (800) 327-8246

Menu

Pickled Herring

Aquavit

A Few French Kisses*

Armagnac-Cooked Prunes Stuffed with *Foie Gras*

French Sauternes—Château d'Yquem

Asparagus and Lemon Pasta with Beluga Caviar

Champagne—Bollinger RD

Heart-Shaped Sun-Dried Tomato Meat Loaves

Mashed Potatoes

California Zinfandel—Ridge Vineyards 1974

Chocolate Climax

A Cocktail Named Desire

Asparagus and Lemon Pasta with Beluga Caviar

1 cup dry white wine

3 tablespoons minced shallots

2 large lemons, zested and juiced

12 ounces fresh fettuccine, cooked
al dente

1½ cups heavy cream

⅓ cup freshly grated Parmesan cheese

4 tablespoons unsalted butter, cold,
cut into small pieces

10 medium asparagus, spears peeled,
blanched (for 1 minute in boiling
water), and cut into ½-inch pieces
on the bias

Salt and cayenne pepper

2 tablespoons finely snipped chives

1 to 2 ounces beluga caviar

> Symbolic asparagus in a lemony smooth sauce served over *al dente* pasta punctuated with a spoonful of slightly salty caviar.

1 POUR THE wine into a large, nonstick skillet set over high heat. Add the shallots and bring to a boil. Lower the heat and cook until the wine is reduced by half, about 5 minutes. Add ½ tablespoon of the zest to the shallots and wine. Add the juice of both lemons and simmer for 2 minutes.

2 COOK THE fettuccine in a large pot of boiling salted water according to the package directions until *al dente*. Drain the pasta well and set aside.

3 WHISK THE cream into the wine and shallot mixture and bring to a boil, stirring constantly. Add the cheese, lower the heat, and simmer until the sauce has thickened, about 4 minutes. Add the butter and stir until it is incorporated, about 2 minutes. Stir in the blanched asparagus and cooked pasta and toss well. Season with salt and cayenne to taste. Cook briefly over medium heat until hot.

4 SERVE THE pasta in heated flat soup plates. Mix together the remaining lemon zest and chives and sprinkle over the pasta. Top with a spoonful of caviar and serve at once.

Heart-Shaped Sun-Dried Tomato Meat Loaves

One 8-ounce jar oil-packed sun-dried tomatoes, drained, diced, and oil reserved

1 large yellow onion, finely diced

1½ pounds top-quality ground sirloin

Salt and freshly ground black pepper

Catsup

Parsley sprigs, for garnish

1 PREHEAT THE oven to 350°F. Line a heavy, rimmed baking tray with aluminum foil and set aside.

2 POUR 3 tablespoons of the sun-dried tomato oil into a nonstick skillet set over medium heat. Add the onion and cook until soft but not brown, about 10 minutes.

3 COMBINE THE sirloin, dried tomatoes, and onion mixture. Stir in ¼ cup cold water and add 1 teaspoon salt and ½ teaspoon pepper. Mix thoroughly.

4 PLACE THE meat on the prepared baking pan and, using your hands, form it into 2 heart shapes. Bake until crisp and brown on the outside, according to your preference, about 30 minutes. Let rest 5 minutes before serving. Serve with catsup and garnish the plates with a sprig of parsley.

Chocolate Climax

5 ounces excellent semisweet
    chocolate, chopped into small
    pieces
5 tablespoons unsalted butter, cold,
    cut into cubes

2 extra large eggs, at room
    temperature
Pinch salt
Whipped Cream (see page 14)

Whipped Cream (see page 14)

> Served chilled but not too cold, these little cakes are creamy and almost fudgelike.

1 PREHEAT THE oven to 425°F. Butter 6 small ramekins. Partially fill a large roasting pan with water and set it in the oven.

2 PLACE THE chopped chocolate and the butter into a metal mixing bowl set over barely simmering water. Melt until the mixture is completely smooth, stirring occasionally, about 4 minutes. Remove from the heat and cool for 3 minutes.

3 BEAT THE eggs with a pinch of salt until they become soft peaks, about 5 minutes. Using a wire whisk, fold half of the beaten eggs into the melted chocolate and mix well, then fold in the remaining eggs, mixing thoroughly.

4 POUR THE batter into the prepared ramekins and set them in the pan of hot water. Add enough simmering water to reach up to the level of the batter. Cover the entire pan with buttered aluminum foil, buttered-side down. Bake for 5 minutes, then remove the foil and bake for 9 minutes longer. Carefully remove the cakes from the water bath and let them cool to room temperature for at least 3 hours. They will continue to set as they cool. Refrigerate the ramekins if they are not to be served within 4 hours. (Return to room temperature before unmolding.) Unmold two ramekins onto a large serving platter and top each with a dollop of whipped cream.

A Cocktail Named Desire

2 ounces Irish whiskey
2 ounces Irish Mist liqueur

About ⅓ cup *unsweetened* heavy cream, lightly whipped

POUR THE spirits into a mixing glass over lots of ice. Stir briskly, strain into 2 chilled cocktail glasses, and spoon ½ inch of whipped cream over the top to cover.

"FOOD BROUGHT US together," says Vincent Guérithault of his wife, Leevon, whom he met when she hired him to cater one of her company's parties in 1986. Together they have built a Franco-Southwest oasis in the desert. With a thriving business and three children, the only romantic get-aways Vincent has are in his memory. He remembers the time when he took Leevon for a drive to Oak Creek Canyon, en route to Sedona, to have a picnic lunch. "The winding road along the canyon was gorgeous," Vincent says, recalling the blue sky and red clay mountains. "We sat beside a creek and enjoyed chilled lobsters and champagne. I even brought roses." For Vincent, the most difficult part was not impressing his date but rather carrying the ice chest down into the canyon. "It was very heavy." Instead of picnics in the canyon, the couple now settle for a cozy table outside in the restaurant's hideaway garden, where they can nibble on Smoked Salmon Quesadillas and Grilled Lobster with Chipotle Pasta.

Vincent Guérithault

Vincent Guérithault on Camelback

Phoenix, Arizona

Menu

Smoked Salmon Quesadillas

Champagne—Moët & Chandon, Brut Rosé, NV

Grilled Lobster with *Chipotle* Pasta

California Viognier—Calera Wine Co., Mount Harlan, 1997

Ambrosial Orange Sauce with Berries and Pound Cake

French Muscat de Beaumes-de-Venise—
Domaine de Coyeux, 1997

Smoked Salmon Quesadillas

If you've little time
to cook, but wish to
entertain that certain
someone, ice a bottle of
your favorite
champagne, whip up
these heavenly
quesadillas, and then go
out for dinner. Or
maybe just finish the
champagne and go for
a sunset stroll.

For the horseradish cream

⅓ cup mild goat cheese

1 tablespoon grated fresh horseradish

1 tablespoon sour cream

1 teaspoon chopped dill

Salt and freshly ground black pepper

For the quesadillas

2 tablespoons olive oil

Four 8-inch flour tortillas

4 thin slices smoked salmon

Chopped dill, for garnish

1 BLEND THE goat cheese, horseradish, sour cream, and dill together in a food processor. Taste and season with salt and pepper.

2 COAT WITH oil a nonstick skillet; set over high heat. Set aside. Cook the tortillas until light brown, about 1 minute per side. Transfer to a cutting board and evenly spread about 1 tablespoon of the horseradish cream over each tortilla. Arrange the smoked salmon over the cream and sprinkle with chopped dill. Cut into quarters and serve.

Grilled Lobster with *Chipotle* Pasta

For the pasta
½ cup all-purpose flour
½ tablespoon *chipotle* chiles canned
    in adobo sauce (an imported
    Mexican product available in
    the specialty sections of many
    markets)
1 medium egg

½ teaspoon olive oil
Dash salt

Two 1-pound lobsters
Olive oil, for brushing
About 1½ tablespoons butter
Freshly ground black pepper
About 1 tablespoon chopped fresh
    cilantro, for garnish

Make an art out of eating the lobster, using your hands to crack open those bright red shells and working for that tiny last morsel of meat in the legs. You'll enjoy the combination of the sweet meat and spicy pasta even more.

1 MIX THE flour with the chipotle purée in the bowl of the food processor. Add the egg and mix. Slowly add the olive oil and salt. Process until well mixed and the dough resembles couscous. Add 1 teaspoon water, if necessary. It will not come together in a ball. Dump the dough onto a floured board and knead with the heels of your hands until it is smooth and supple. The dough should not be at all sticky. Continue to work the dough for a few minutes until it is smooth, then cut it into 4 to 5 pieces.

2 SET THE rollers of a pasta machine at the widest setting and feed one of the pieces of dough through the rollers. Fold the dough in half and feed it again through the rollers. Continue to roll and fold each piece of the dough until the pasta "pops" (the air bubble in the fold will pop or snap) to let you know that it's ready.

3 REDUCE THE pasta machine setting, roll the pasta again, and continue rolling, reducing the setting in increments until the pasta is fairly thin. Remove the rollers and attach the cutting blades. Cut into flat ribbon noodles, about ½ to 1 inch wide. Place on a rack to dry. Store refrigerated in a plastic bag overnight, if necessary.

4 PREHEAT THE grill until the coals are white hot. Halve the lobsters lengthwise and remove the stomach and veins. Brush the insides of the lobster with olive oil and grill, meat side down first, for 7 to 8 minutes. Turn the lobster over and grill for 5 minutes longer. Set the lobster on a board and crack open the claws. Transfer to a warm plate.

5 BRING ABOUT 3 quarts of salted water to a boil in a large saucepan set over high heat. When the lobster is nearly done, cook the pasta until *al dente,* 1 to 2 minutes. Drain the pasta. Divide the pasta between two warm bowls, dress with butter, and season with pepper to taste. Sprinkle with cilantro and serve with the lobster.

Ambrosial Orange Sauce

¼ cup heavy cream

2 oranges, zested and juiced

1 lemon, zested and juiced

3 tablespoons sugar

2 tablespoons butter

1 WHIP THE cream until it has body and consistency but is not stiff. Set aside.

2 COMBINE THE zest (about 2 tablespoons) and the juices (about ⅔ cup) of the oranges and lemon in a nonreactive saucepan over high heat and bring to a boil. Add the sugar and stir until dissolved. Reduce the heat to medium and gently blend in the butter and cream. Cook, stirring frequently, until the liquid is reduced to one-third of its volume. Transfer to a pitcher and cool to room temperature.

3 TO SERVE, pour over fresh berries and pound cake or ice cream.

Chef Guérithault serves this sauce with a soufflé, but, if the notion of having a soufflé flop is too scary, prepare only the orange sauce and serve it with strawberries. It also makes fingers taste better!

YEARS AGO WHEN Gordon spotted Fiona, a slim, blond beauty with pool-blue eyes, as she was stepping out of a red Ferrari in Los Angeles, he knew it was all over. "I just said, 'Wow! I have to have that!'" The red Ferrari? "Well, that would have been a lot less work and a lot less expensive in the long run!" Gordon bursts into laughter as Fiona leans over and playfully slaps her husband's knee. This dashing couple loves to laugh. Partners not only in life but also in Hamersley's Bistro, an award-winning restaurant.

It all began when he was the executive sous-chef and she was the catering director of a hotel restaurant in California. "It was her job to book weddings and other affairs, and it was my job to produce whatever she decided the menu was going to be. She would meet the clients and say, 'Whatever you want to eat is fine with us,'" Gordon complains, "even something like individual frozen soufflés for an outdoor affair in the middle of July. Then she would present me with these menus and I'd slap my forehead and say, 'You've got to be kidding!'"

These two decided to keep things relatively low key for their own nuptials by surprising Gordon's relatives at a family gathering. While Gordon and Fiona prepared a dinner of scallops and quail with leeks, a dozen relatives as well as a Justice of the Peace, who was a friend of the host, enjoyed cocktails. No one suspected a thing. "His cousin made a toast. 'Gordon and Fiona have put together this dinner, the Cardinals are in the World Series, and they have decided to make it a triple header by getting married!' The Justice of the Peace, who had been knocking back Scotches, staggered over and married us. Then we put our aprons back on and served dinner. Afterward, we all watched the World Series."

Menu

Scallops with Red Curry and Chickpeas

Alsatian Riesling—Trimbach Cuvée Frédéric-Emile, 1993

Pan-Seared Chicken Breast with Leeks and Star Anise

California Sparkling Wine—Schramsberg Vineyards, Brut Rosé, 1994

Fresh Strawberries

French Sauternes—Château Guiraud, 1988 or California Sémillon—Chalk Hill Winery, 1994

Scallops with Red Curry and Chickpeas

¼ cup dry white wine

1 shallot, minced

¼ cup heavy cream

¼ cup coconut milk

¼ teaspoon cayenne pepper

¼ cup Thai red curry paste

Dash Thai fish sauce (*nam pla*)

Olive oil

1 pound sea scallops, washed, patted
   dry with paper towels, and trimmed

¾ cup cooked (or canned) drained
   chickpeas

¾ cup green peas, defrosted and
   drained

4 celery leaves, chopped

Salt and freshly ground black pepper

Cooked jasmine rice, for serving

1 BOIL THE wine and shallot in a saucepan set over high heat, cooking until the liquid is reduced to about 1 tablespoon. Pour in the cream and bring to a boil again. Lower the heat and simmer until the cream begins to thicken slightly, about 5 minutes.

2 ADD THE coconut milk, cayenne, curry paste, and fish sauce and bring the sauce to a boil. Remove from the heat, taste, and correct the seasonings.

3 COAT A skillet with olive oil and set it over high heat. Add the scallops and brown on one side, 1 to 2 minutes for rare, sear on the other side for about 1 minute, remove from the pan, and keep warm. Add the chickpeas, green peas, and celery leaves to the pan and cook over high heat, shaking the pan back and forth, for 1 minute. Add the sauce and cook until the flavors are blended, adding salt and pepper to taste, about 3 minutes.

4 SPOON A mound of jasmine rice in the center of each plate and arrange the scallops around the rice. If there is scallop juice left from the holding plate, whisk it into the sauce. Spoon the sauce with its vegetables around the plate and over the scallops. Serve at once.

Melt-in-your-mouth scallops are staples among Don Juans. The spices in Thai red curry paste and the fish sauce perk up this dish, while chickpeas and green peas dressed with a creamy coconut-based sauce mellow it. Scallops served in this fashion are likely to turn a timid friend into an avid admirer.

Pan-Seared Chicken Breast
with Leeks and Star Anise

⅛ teaspoon ground mace
⅛ teaspoon ground cinnamon
2 whole star anise
¼ cup soy sauce
¼ cup medium-dry sherry
1 teaspoon chopped fresh ginger
½ teaspoon chopped garlic
½ teaspoon coriander seeds, toasted
¼ cup sesame oil
¼ teaspoon coarsely ground black pepper

½ cup orange juice
Freshly ground black pepper
2 whole chicken breasts, with skin and bones, split in half and breast bone removed
2 medium leeks, cleaned, trimmed, and whites cut into ¼-inch rounds
¼ cup olive oil
Salad greens, for serving

1 MIX TOGETHER the mace, cinnamon, star anise, soy sauce, sherry, ginger, garlic, coriander, sesame oil, pepper, and orange juice. Let the flavors blend for at least 30 minutes. Marinate the chicken in half the spice and orange juice mixture for about 30 minutes, drain, and discard the marinade.

2 MEANWHILE, BRING a large pot of salted water to a boil and blanch the leeks for 1 minute. Drain and rinse in cold water, drain well, and reserve.

3 WHISK THE olive oil into the remainder of the marinade and reserve it for a sauce and salad dressing.

4 COAT WITH olive oil a large heavy skillet; set over high heat. Place the chicken, skin-side down in the skillet, and cook until browned, about 4 minutes. Turn over and continue cooking until brown on both sides, about 5 minutes longer. Reduce the heat to medium, add a splash of the reserved marinade, lightly cover with aluminum foil, and continue cooking until the juices run clear when the meat is poked with a meat fork, about 10 minutes. When done, transfer the chicken to a plate and keep warm.

5 COOK THE leeks in the same skillet, stirring, until barely cooked, about 3 minutes.

6 TO SERVE, spoon the leek mixture onto warm dinner plates. Place one piece of chicken breast on each plate and spoon a bit of the marinade over. Serve with salad greens that have been lightly dressed with the reserved marinade.

David Paul Johnson

David Paul's Lahaina Grill

Maui, Hawaii

DAVID PAUL JOHNSON met his future wife, Michelle, at his best friend's wedding, having just broken off a seven-year relationship. "Staying single and having fun were at the top of my priority list," says David. But, after spotting Michelle, he turned to his friend and said the proverbial line, "That's the woman I'm going to marry."

On their first date, Michelle wanted David to cook her dinner. He was a little wary but took her back to his house anyway. He prepared a delicious rack of lamb, which happily turned out to be Michelle's favorite. After dinner, they sat outside on his dock overlooking the water bathed in full moonlight (no, this is not made up), and that's when he knew. "I fell in love with her right there. I just looked into her eyes and saw my future."

Bachelorhood wasn't going to give up David without a fight. He lied, cheated, anything to avoid admitting the inevitable—that he was hopelessly in love. "Giving up your freedom is hard, but the rewards of having that woman as your best friend, your soul mate, and the mother of your children far outweigh freedom any day. Dating is such a drag. It's so draining having to find out whether or not this or that person is right for you, especially for chefs who work seventeen-hour days six or seven days a week. We don't have the time to spend with someone who isn't right. It's like eating a bad meal and life's too short to eat bad meals."

For David, his culinary skills are his way of giving honeymooners and locals not only delicious Pacific Rim specialties but also *Aloha,* which means greetings, goodbye, and love in Hawaii. To express this feeling, he'll frequently plant kisses on both of their cheeks. "Sometimes, I get stunned looks from people, but it is my way of welcoming them."

Menu

Toy Box (baby) Tomato Salad

Signorello Sauvignon Blanc

Pepper-Seared Medallions of Pork
with Zinfandel-Vanilla Sauce and Jasmine Rice

California White Zinfandel

Triple Berry Pie

Port—A. A. Ferreira, Quinta do Vesuvio

Pepper-Seared Medallions of Pork with Zinfandel-Vanilla Sauce and Jasmine Rice

1 tablespoon olive oil

Juice of half a lemon

4 or 5 sprigs fresh thyme and
    rosemary

1 whole tenderloin of pork,
    about 1½ pounds

2 cups Zinfandel wine

2 vanilla beans, split in half lengthwise

2 cups veal Demi-Glace Gold

2 tablespoons softened butter

1 medium shallot, chopped

1 teaspoon chopped fresh thyme

½ cup jasmine rice, washed and well
    drained

1½ cups chicken stock, boiling

Coarse salt

About ¼ cup freshly cracked black
    pepper

For this recipe less is more. Three ingredients are reduced to create an alluring vanilla-scented rich brown sauce that's spooned over the pork. Time and patience are the most important ingredients. If you like *foie gras*, sear two ½-inch-thick slices to garnish the pork.

1 COMBINE THE olive oil, lemon juice, and 2 sprigs each of fresh thyme and rosemary in a bowl. Add the tenderloin and coat with the marinade. Cover and let stand for 30 minutes.

2 IN A large, nonreactive saucepan set over high heat, combine the wine, 1 of the vanilla beans, and the demi-glace. Reduce the heat to low and cook until the mixture is syrupy, reduced by half, and the sauce coats the back of a spoon, 30 to 35 minutes. Remove the vanilla bean.

3 IN A heavy-bottomed saucepan set over moderately high heat, melt the butter and cook the shallot, chopped thyme, and the second vanilla bean, stirring, until the shallot is softened, about 3 minutes. Add the rice and stir until it glistens, about 2 minutes. Add the stock and bring to a boil. Reduce the heat, cover, and simmer until all the liquid is absorbed, about 20 minutes. Remove from the heat, remove the vanilla bean, and fluff with a fork. Add salt and pepper to taste. Set aside. *continued*

4 PREHEAT THE oven to 450°F. Remove the tenderloin from the marinade. Pat the meat dry with paper towels and season with coarse salt and lots of freshly cracked pepper. In a very hot, heavy skillet set over high heat, sear all sides of the tenderloin. Remove the pork to a small roasting pan. Add a splash of Zinfandel and a splash of stock to the hot skillet, stir for 30 seconds, and pour the mixture over the tenderloin. Place the tenderloin in the oven and roast until the desired doneness, about 20 minutes. Remove from the oven and let stand for 10 minutes.

5 CUT THE tenderloin into 2-inch-thick medallions and arrange them on warm dinner plates. Ladle about 2 tablespoons of sauce over and around the pork, spoon a serving of rice on the side, and garnish with the remaining sprigs of rosemary and thyme.

Love Note: Use Demi-Glace Gold for the sauce. Follow the directions on the label. To order, contact:

Demi-Glace Gold
More than Gourmet
115 West Bartges Street
Akron, OH 44311
(330) 762-6652

Triple Berry Pie

For the crust

3 cups all-purpose flour

2 tablespoons sugar

½ teaspoon salt

1 cup (2 sticks) cold, unsalted butter,
    cut into pieces

6 tablespoons sour cream

6 tablespoons ice water, or more if
    necessary

12 ounces raspberries, frozen

12 ounces blueberries, frozen

12 ounces fresh black currants,
    washed and picked over, or
    strawberries, or blackberries

¼ cup crème de cassis

1 teaspoon pure vanilla extract

¼ cup tapioca

1 cup sugar

2 tablespoons butter, cut into small
    pieces

1 large egg, beaten with a teaspoon of
    water (egg wash)

1 MAKE THE dough 6 hours before serving. Mix the flour, sugar, and salt together in a food processor. Add the butter and pulse until the mixture looks like coarse meal. Transfer the flour mixture to a mixing bowl. Stir in the sour cream and then the water until combined. Add more water if necessary to make a ball of pastry. Wrap in plastic and chill for 1 hour.

2 FOR THE filling, combine the raspberries, blueberries, and black currants with the cassis and vanilla. Combine the tapioca and the sugar and stir into the berry mixture. Reserve the filling in the freezer.

3 DIVIDE THE dough in half. Working on a floured surface, roll each half out to a circle about 11 inches in diameter and ⅛ inch thick. Grease the bottom of a 9-inch pie pan and place one crust in the pan, leaving a ½-inch overhang around the edges. Spoon the frozen berry mixture into the pie shell. Dot the top of the berries with 2 tablespoons of the chopped butter.

continued

This pie was created during a crime of passion. "My wife," David explains, "kidnapped me and took me to a cabin in the mountains of Kauai. I wasn't allowed to bring my laptop or my cellular phone, just magazines. I was trying to create a Valentine's Day dessert and started reading about pies. Pies are romantic because they give you a warm and fuzzy, nurturing feeling." This recipe serves 8 to 10 people, but leftover pie is great for breakfast.

Roll out the second crust and place it on top. Being sure to overlap the edges, fold the overhanging edge of the bottom crust up, over the top crust, and crimp it firmly with your fingers. Freeze the pie for 1 hour.

4 PREHEAT THE oven to 375°F. Cut a small hole in the top crust at the center of the pie. Brush the pie with egg wash and dust with sugar. After 1 hour, reduce the heat to 350°F and continue to bake the pie until the crust is brown on top and the filling in the center of the pie is bubbling, 30 to 45 minutes longer. Remove from the oven and set the pie on a rack for 1 hour. When completely cool, cut into serving-size portions and serve topped with fresh berries and Whipped Cream (page 14).

Anne Kearney

Peristyle

New Orleans, Louisiana

SOMETIMES PRINCES DO come. For Anne Kearney, the beautiful blond proprietor of Peristyle in New Orleans, the fairy tale began one night during a holiday visit to her hometown of Dayton, Ohio. In a bar with her sister, she spotted Tom—an old crush from high school. Suddenly, she was a teenager again, feeling awkward and too shy to approach him. Her sister forced her to say hello. Back in New Orleans, Anne received a "I've-never-written-a-letter-like-this-in-my-life" letter from Tom. She wrote back telling him that she would return to Dayton soon, and an official first date was made.

Tom took her to a wine and cigar jazz bar. Over a bottle of Chardonnay (they still have the cork), they talked about their dreams and the importance of family and realized that they were cut from the same cloth. Anne recalls what has become affectionately known in her family as "The Kiss." "It was snowing. We were standing under a gazebo and we could still hear the music playing from inside the bar. I was telling him what a great time I had when he swung me around in his arms and kissed me. It was one of those moments that everyone waits for in their lifetimes."

When it came time to celebrate their engagement, Anne prepared a family dinner called the Dinner of Love and served everyone's favorite dishes. She pulled out all the stops including printed menus and even baby pictures in lieu of place cards. She served oyster soup for her mother and grilled lamb loin for Tom. "I was really trying to win them over. I wanted everyone to be intoxicated by how much I love Tom and how much he loves me."

The newlyweds settled down in New Orleans to run their Provençal bistro together. Above the porthole window of the kitchen door, Anne hand painted a sign, Food of Love, as a constant reminder of the lifelong passion that she devotes to every plate that passes through the door.

Menu

California Chardonnay—Far Niente, 1994

Grilled Loin of Lamb With Red Wine Sauce

Walnut-Crusted Celeriac and Potato Gratin

Pinot noir—Domaine Serene, Evanstead Reserve,
Willamette, Oregon, 1994

Sliced Fresh Pears

France—Pineau des Charentes, Pierre Ferrand Reserve

Grilled Loin of Lamb with
Red Wine Sauce

An elegant and flavorful entrée, this lamb dish is simple to execute if you start the preparation early in the day. Slip on rubber gloves to spread the sweet and spicy rub onto the meat, then refrigerate it. The sauce can also be cooked ahead of time by combining Demi-Glace Gold (diluted according to the directions on the package) and red wine with shallots. Save leftover sauce for another dinner.

For the sauce

1 cup dry red wine
1 cup rich veal stock (Demi-Glace Gold, see page 100)
2 shallots, chopped

1 teaspoon chopped fresh thyme
About 1 tablespoon unsalted butter, softened

For the rub

1 clove garlic, peeled
2 tablespoons peanut oil
1 tablespoon mango chutney
1 teaspoon sambal (Indonesian chile paste)
1 teaspoon ground cumin, toasted (page 12)

1 teaspoon ground fennel seed, toasted (page 12)
Pinch white pepper

Two 8-ounce boneless loins of lamb, fat and silverskin removed

1 TO MAKE the sauce, combine the wine, veal stock, shallots, and thyme in a nonreactive saucepan. Cover, bring to a boil over high heat, and then cook until reduced by half. Strain out the shallots and herbs, return the sauce to a clean saucepan, and bring to a simmer. Cook for 10 minutes longer and set aside (or store for up to 6 hours refrigerated).

2 TO MAKE the rub, place the garlic, oil, chutney, *sambal*, cumin, fennel, and pepper in a blender or food processor and purée until smooth.

3 PAT THE meat dry with paper towels, then apply the rub with your hands, really rubbing it into the meat. Cover the meat with plastic and refrigerate for up to 6 hours.

4 PREHEAT A grill until the coals are white hot or, to pan-sear the lamb, set a heavy sauté pan over high heat. Just before cooking the meat, scrape off excess marinade (rub) from the lamb and sprinkle the meat with salt and freshly ground black pepper to taste; this will give it a nice brown crust. Grill the meat or sear it until it is brown on all the sides, cooking for about 4 to 5 minutes to serve rare or cook until the desired doneness. Let the meat rest in a warm place for 5 to 6 minutes.

5 IN THE same sauté pan (or a saucepan if the meat is grilled), bring ½ cup of the red wine sauce to a boil over high heat. Off the heat, swirl in the butter.

6 CUT THE lamb into ¼- to ½-inch-thick medallions. Arrange the medallions on warm dinner plates, ladle the sauce over, and serve with Walnut-Crusted Celeriac and Potato Gratin (recipe follows).

Walnut-Crusted Celeriac and Potato Gratin

¼ cup heavy cream

1 large Idaho potato, peeled

Salt and freshly ground black pepper

¼ cup freshly grated Parmesan cheese

8 ounces (about 1½ cups) peeled
    celeriac (celery root—1 medium
    bulb)

¼ cup coarse dry bread crumbs

¼ cup chopped walnuts, toasted

About 2 teaspoons extra virgin olive
    oil

1 PREHEAT THE oven to 375°F. Line a 1-quart baking dish with parchment paper. Drizzle a thin layer of cream on the bottom of the dish.

2 SLICE THE potato thinly (a slicer or mandoline makes this a simple task) and line the bottom of the dish with potatoes. Sprinkle on some salt and pepper and add a thin layer of cream and a sprinkling of cheese. Repeat until you have four thin layers of potatoes, each seasoned with salt, pepper, cream, and cheese. Then thinly slice the celeriac on the mandoline and make four similar layers each seasoned with salt, pepper, cream, and cheese. Repeat the layering process until you have no more potatoes and celeriac. Work quickly to prevent the potatoes from discoloring and gently press down the layers as you go.

3 COMBINE THE bread crumbs and nuts together with oil. Press the mixture evenly over the gratin. Cover with foil and bake for 1 hour, or until the potatoes are tender to the point of a fork. Remove the foil and brown the top until golden, about 15 to 20 minutes. Let the gratin rest for 10 minutes before cutting and serving it.

A SUNDAY DRIVE through the Hudson Valley with your honey, stopping to peek into antique shops or pick apples off trees, is an enchanting way to spend the day. If you are searching for a field of dreams, turn onto Shaker Museum Road, go past the green pastures dotted with cotton-ball sheep, and pull up to the buttery yellow Georgian manor house. You've arrived at the Old Chatham Sheepherding Company Inn.

Fall into each other's arms on a quilt-covered bed in one of the rooms packed with Early American furniture and decorative antiques. Rise and shine to the sound of baa-ing sheep and head to the dining room where young Melissa Kelly will feed you baked breads, muffins, and sheep's milk yogurt fresh from the inn's farm.

On Valentine's Day, Melissa offers a menu of dishes filled with aphrodisiacs, such as lobster with vanilla butter and fig, artichoke, and wild mushroom risotto. "I like to pair aphrodisiacs together," she says.

In the summer, guests travel to Tanglewood for an evening of music under the stars. Last year, Melissa and her fiancé, Price, a baker at the inn, packed up their picnic basket and made the trip for the James Taylor concert. They brought the usual romantic staples, champagne and caviar, along with a few specialties, candles, and a nice cozy blanket.

Picnics, Melissa believes, are a great first-date activity. "A picnic in the country is incredibly romantic. The trick is to keep everything simple and beautiful. If you are going to go through the trouble, make it worth your while," she says. "Spend the money on a picnic basket. Don't carry a cardboard box or a paper bag. And take wine glasses or enamelware, instead of Dixie cups."

Melissa Kelly

Old Chatham
Sheepherding Company
Inn

Old Chatham, New York

Menu

A two-ounce tin of osetra caviar served with sliced hard-boiled eggs, chopped red onion, toast points, crème fraîche, and fresh chives

A selection of cheeses—Camembert, *pecorino di noci*—Montbriac—served with fresh figs, French baguettes, and apples

Rosemary-Roasted Almonds

Cured meats: prosciutto, sopressata

Stewed Artichokes with Lemon Aïoli

Field greens served with fresh sheep's cheese

Glazed Summer Berry Tartlets

Champagne

Rosemary-Roasted Almonds

These rosemary-flavored almonds are nearly addictive, so pack enough to nibble on the way to the picnic. Walnuts or pecans are just as delicious.

2 cups whole almonds, shelled but not peeled

¼ cup extra virgin olive oil

1½ tablespoons chopped fresh rosemary, or 2 teaspoons dried

½ teaspoon finely minced garlic

¼ teaspoon crushed red pepper

Coarse salt and freshly ground black pepper

1 PREHEAT the oven to 350°F.

2 PLACE THE almonds in a shallow pan and bake until they become aromatic and toasted but not brown, about 20 minutes.

3 WHISK TOGETHER the olive oil, rosemary, garlic, and crushed red pepper in a large stainless steel bowl. Add the nuts and toss well. Taste and adjust the seasonings, adding salt and pepper to taste. Let cool.

4 STORE IN an airtight container for up to 2 months. Serve with an apéritif, cheese, or antipasto.

Love Note: These nuts make great hostess gifts, so if you are going to your lover's house take some along!

Stewed Artichokes with Lemon Aïoli

2 medium-sized globe artichokes

Juice of 2 lemons, separated

½ cup dry white wine

1 bay leaf

1 sprig fresh basil

½ teaspoon whole coriander seeds

¼ teaspoon whole black peppercorns

3 cloves garlic, smashed

½ cup extra virgin olive oil

For the aïoli

2 medium egg yolks

2 teaspoons Dijon mustard

Zest of 1 large lemon

2 small cloves garlic, finely minced

¾ cup olive oil

1 to 1½ tablespoons fresh lemon juice

Coarse salt and freshly ground white
  pepper

1 PREHEAT the oven to 400°F. Trim off the top thorny tips of the artichokes with a pair of scissors. Trim off the bottom of the stem and the outer layer of skin around the bottom with a sharp knife, leaving about 1 inch of the stem. Rub lemon juice over each artichoke before trimming the next one.

2 PLACE THE artichokes upside down in a large, deep, nonreactive casserole dish, add the wine, lemon juice, bay leaf, basil, coriander seeds, peppercorns, garlic, and olive oil. Add enough water to cover. Cover and bake until the bottoms are tender to the point of a knife, about 1 hour. Remove from the liquid, drain for a few minutes, and serve warm with dipping sauce on the side.

3 TO PREPARE the aïoli, process the egg yolks and mustard in a food processor or blender until well mixed. Add the lemon zest and garlic. With the machine running, drizzle the olive oil through the feeding tube, in a very thin stream until the mixture becomes thick, the consistency of a mayonnaise. Continue adding oil and lemon juice alternately once the sauce begins to thicken. Mix until emulsified. Add salt and pepper to taste.

The seductive art of eating an artichoke: Dip each light green piece that you have peeled from the bulb into the creamy garlic sauce and use your teeth and lips to remove the vegetable meat and sauce from the shell of the leaf.

Glazed Summer Berry Tartlets

The secret to these tarts lies in the addition of mascarpone cheese, an Italian buttery-rich cheese that makes these tartlets something like cheesecakes, only much more delicate.

For the crust

2 cups all-purpose flour

¼ cup sugar

Pinch salt

6 ounces (1½ sticks) cold, unsalted
   butter, cut into pieces

1 large egg

1 large egg yolk

For the filling

½ cup heavy cream

½ teaspoon pure vanilla extract

2 teaspoons superfine sugar

4 ounces mascarpone

1½ cups assorted fresh berries:
   raspberries, blackberries,
   strawberries, picked over, washed,
   and well drained

For the glaze

⅓ cup apricot jam

2 tablespoons water

1 PREPARE THE crust 1 day ahead. Place the flour, sugar, and salt into a food processor and pulse until mixed. Cut the cold butter into the flour until the mixture resembles coarse meal. Do not overprocess. Transfer the mixture to a mixing bowl, make a well in the center, place the egg and egg yolk in the well, and mix with a fork until the dough comes together in a ball. Add a splash or two of cold water if necessary. Wrap the dough in plastic and chill for at least 1 hour.

2 PREHEAT THE oven to 350°F. Have on hand 5 or 6 tart molds (2½ to 3 inches across) and a large baking sheet.

3 ROLL OUT the dough on a lightly floured board until it is ¼ inch thick. Cut the dough into circles large enough to fit into the tart molds and place the dough in the pans, pressing the edges to crimp onto the sides.

Prick the shell with a fork, cover with plastic wrap, and freeze until firm, about 30 minutes or overnight. Remove the plastic wrap, cover the tart shells with circles of parchment paper, weight the shells down with beans or rice, and bake for 10 minutes. Remove the paper and the beans and continue baking until the shells are a light golden brown and completely done, about 15 minutes longer. Set on a rack and cool completely.

4 FOR THE filling, whip the cream until soft peaks form, add the vanilla and sugar and mix well. In a separate bowl, whisk the mascarpone cheese to lighten it and then fold it into the cream. Taste and correct the sweetness.

5 IN A small microwave-proof bowl, melt the apricot jam together with the water and set aside. Fill each pastry shell with mascarpone mixture, top with pretty berries, and then, using a pastry brush, brush the glaze on the berries. Refrigerate until serving time.

Peter Xaviar Kelly

Xaviar's

Garrison and Piermont,
New York

XAVIAR'S IN GARRISON sits grandly on a hill surrounded by an expanse of golf greens at the Highlands Country Club. (Its more intimate baby sister lives in Piermont, a picturesque community along the Hudson River.)

When the chef he hired for Xaviar's proved to be inadequate, Peter Kelly locked himself in his kitchen with an armful of cookbooks to learn the secrets from masters such as Jacques Pépin and Julia Child. Through trial and error (and a few minor catastrophes), he emerged good enough to keep Westchesterites in town instead of driving into Manhattan for a classic French four-star dinner.

Elegance is very important to Kelly. The restaurant is dipped in luxury—Versace china, fresh flowers arranged in Waterford crystal, Baccarat figurines, and Cartier salt and pepper shakers. To prepare an intimate and elaborate dinner at home, the chef suggests using elements that are found in his restaurants such as candles, fresh flowers, fine china, and linens. "Invest in good linen napkins. After all, you are going to be touching your face with them." But big expensive floral arrangements are not always necessary. "Try a single bud on the table or even an orchid floating in a wine glass."

If you don't have the time or the inclination to prepare an extravagant table and meal, Kelly would recommend a shellfish platter or a simple crab boil, something he used to eat with his "first and last" wife, Rica. "When we were courting, I would bring her a cold plate of shellfish, and we would sit, eating seafood and watching movies until midnight."

Any last words of wisdom before you attempt this feast? "If you are going to make the rib eye," and here Kelly lowers his voice, "make sure she's not a vegetarian."

Menu

Glazed Double-Cut Rib-Eye Steak with Caramelized Shallots

Cabernet Sauvignon—Behurens & Hitchcock,
Inkgrade Vineyard, Napa, California, 1995

Raspberry Napoleons

Hungarian Tokay—Tokaji Aszú (6 *puttonyos*), Orimus, 1981

Glazed Double-Cut Rib-Eye Steak with Caramelized Shallots

2 tablespoons brown sugar

1 teaspoon Dijon mustard

1 rib-eye steak, well trimmed, bone in, and cut 2½ inches thick

For the shallots

¼ cup sugar

10 large shallots, peeled

Salt and freshly cracked black pepper

⅓ cup balsamic vinegar

½ cup beef stock

A tangy sweet glaze seems unlikely for beef but, once you've tasted it, you'll ask for this combination often, especially when it is accompanied by caramelized shallots.

1 WHISK TOGETHER the brown sugar and mustard. Sprinkle the steak with salt and pepper and rub with the mustard mixture. Cover the steak with plastic wrap and refrigerate for 3 hours or overnight.

2 FOR THE caramelized shallots, preheat the oven to 400°F. Set an ovenproof casserole dish over medium heat, add the sugar, and melt until it caramelizes, becoming a dark amber color; be careful not to burn it. Quickly add the shallots, vinegar, and beef stock, stirring with a wooden spoon, until the liquid is smooth. Increase the heat, bring to a boil, and reduce the liquid until it is just slightly syrupy, about 3 minutes.

3 PLACE THE casserole in the oven and cook until the shallots are tender, about 20 minutes. Reserve.

4 HEAT THE grill until the coals are white hot or heat a grill pan until it is very hot. Sear the steak for 3 minutes on each side to create a nice charred exterior. Continue grilling, turning often, for about 6 minutes for medium rare. If you like your steak well cooked, continue grilling until done (when a slice into the steak reveals the color your heart desires). Let the steak rest in a warm place for 10 minutes. Slice and serve on warm plates with the shallots.

Raspberry Napoleons

4 sheets phyllo dough

½ cup unsalted butter, melted

3-inch heart-shaped cookie cutter

¾ cup sugar

2 pints raspberries (reserve 1 pint for
    garnish), washed and picked over

¼ cup Framboise liqueur

1 cup heavy cream

1 teaspoon pure vanilla extract

Pastry bag fitted with a star tip

1 PREHEAT THE oven to 350°F.

2 WORKING ON a clean flat surface, layer 4 sheets of the phyllo dough on top of one another, brushing each sheet with melted butter before you lay the next sheet down on top of it. Using a heart-shaped cookie cutter, cut the phyllo into 6 or 8 individual hearts (2 extra in case of a broken heart!).

3 LINE A cookie sheet with parchment paper and generously sprinkle with sugar. Place the phyllo hearts on the parchment and sprinkle more sugar on top of the cookies. Cover the cookies with another sheet of parchment paper and weight it down with a second cookie sheet. Bake until light brown, about 10 minutes.

4 IN A food processor or blender, purée 1 pint of the raspberries with the liqueur and strain out the seeds. Reserve 3 or 4 tablespoons for garnishing.

5 WHIP THE cream with 2 tablespoons of the sugar and the vanilla until stiff peaks form. Fold all but the reserved raspberry purée into the whipped cream. Fill a pastry bag fitted with a star tip with the mousse and refrigerate if not assembling the dessert immediately.

6 ASSEMBLE THE dessert just before serving, using 3 cookies per person. Place a cooled phyllo cookie in the center of a dessert plate. Pipe some of the raspberry mousse on top of the cookie. Place another cookie on top of the mousse and pipe more mousse over that. Place a third cookie on top and pipe raspberry mousse over it. Drizzle the reserved raspberry purée and the remaining 1 pint fresh raspberries around the plate to garnish. Serve at once.

ACCORDING TO GEORGE Germon, his wife Johanne Killeen has to cook a red sauce for him at least once a week. "It's in our wedding vows," he jokes. As co-owners of the acclaimed Al Forno Restaurant, "I do 60 percent and he does 60 percent," says Johanne, who is in charge of desserts—individually made to order—while her husband produces entrées such as their celebrated grilled pizzas and oven-baked pasta dishes.

Johanne Killeen
and
George Germon

Al Forno

Providence, Rhode Island

Both are trained as artists. It was at the Rhode Island School of Design that Johanne, studying photography, and George, teaching sculpture, first met. But it wasn't until years later, while they were working at the same restaurant, that their romance bloomed.

Since the birth of Al Forno, the couple has spent little time out of the kitchen. It's quite common for them to eat dinner at one o'clock in the morning. "We take our meals seriously. It's the only private time we have together," says Johanne, who affectionately coined their late meals Midnight Spaghetti. The goal is to cook the sauce in as much time as it would take to boil the water for the pasta.

If they could afford the luxury of preparing a romantic dinner before dawn, Johanne and George would share classic dishes that are full of flavor and easy to make. "Italian food is familiar to most people," says Johanne, "and the culture is so lively and full of enjoyment that it's easy to create a celebration with them." If you are feeling overwhelmed, you can take George's advice: "Heavy drinking helps!"

Menu

Spaghetti with Watercress and Garlic

Italian Tocai—*Puiatti* 1997

Roasted Sausages with Grapes

Italian Barbera—*Giacomo Conterno, Barbera d'Alba*, 1997

Fresh Pears with Ginger Yogurt Cheese

Italian Moscato passito—Ivaldi

Spaghetti with Watercress and Garlic

Perfect for two garlic lovers, this light combination of watercress and garlic is almost ready to serve by the time the water for the pasta comes to a boil.

—

¼ cup extra virgin olive oil
1 large clove garlic, minced
Coarse salt
⅔ cup vegetable stock

½ pound spaghetti
1 bunch watercress, tough stems
    removed, leaves coarsely chopped

1 BRING ABOUT 4 quarts of salted water to a boil in a large saucepan set over high heat.

2 HEAT THE olive oil and garlic in a large skillet set over medium heat. Cook, stirring often, until the garlic is golden, about 3 minutes. Season with salt and add the vegetable stock. Bring the liquid to a boil and reduce it by half, about 4 minutes. Reduce the heat to keep the sauce warm.

3 COOK THE spaghetti until barely *al dente,* 4 to 5 minutes. Drain, reserving the cooking water, and add the pasta to the garlic sauce. Add the watercress and toss until the pasta is completely cooked and coated with the oil and garlic, about 2 minutes. Add a splash or two of the pasta cooking water if necessary to create enough sauce. Transfer to two large warm bowls and serve.

Roasted Sausages with Grapes

¼ pound hot Italian sausages

¼ pound sweet Italian sausages

6 large cloves garlic, unpeeled

1½ tablespoons unsalted butter

1 cup red seedless grapes, stems
removed and washed

1 cup green seedless grapes, stems
removed and washed

About 1 tablespoon balsamic vinegar

A fabulous dish to devour in front of the fireplace. Heat a loaf of crusty Italian peasant bread, tear pieces off, and dip them into the juices. Or mound the sausages onto thick slices and serve with a green salad.

1 PREHEAT THE oven to 475°F.

2 PLACE THE sausages and garlic in a large pot, completely cover with cold water, and set over high heat. Bring the water to a boil, reduce the heat, and simmer for 10 minutes. Prick the skin of the sausages to rid them of the excess fat. Drain well.

3 MELT THE butter in a large heavy casserole set over moderate heat, add the grapes, and toss to coat. Transfer the sausages to the casserole dish, pushing them into the grapes. Roast in the oven until the sausages are brown (turning them once) and the grapes are soft, about 20 minutes.

4 TRANSFER THE sausages and grapes to a heated serving platter. Set the casserole on the stove over high heat and add the balsamic vinegar. Stirring up any browned bits in the bottom of the pan, allow the vinegar and juices to reduce until they are thick and syrupy. Spoon the sauce over the sausages and serve at once.

Fresh Pears with Ginger Yogurt Cheese

⅓ cup yogurt cheese (see page 16)

About 1 teaspoon honey, or more to
    taste

1 tablespoon minced crystallized
    ginger

2 perfect ripe pears

About 1 tablespoon fresh orange or
    lemon juice

Sprigs mint, for garnish

1 TO ASSEMBLE the dessert, whisk the yogurt cheese with the honey and ginger. Taste and correct the sweetness.

2 WASH, HALVE, and core the pears. Cut each pear into lengthwise slices, then roll the slices in the orange or lemon juice to prevent their discoloring. Arrange the slices in a spoke fashion on pretty dessert plates. Mound a dollop of yogurt cheese in the center and garnish with mint. Eat the slices of pear with your fingers, dipping the ends into the yogurt cheese.

THE ABUNDANT FLOWERS and magnificent Howard Chandler Christy murals of nude nymphs frolicking in the woods make Café des Artistes the perfect place to fall in love. And in a restaurant where "the question" is popped almost as often as the cork is on a bottle of champagne, it is difficult to be original. One young man was successful when the staff created a special menu for his girlfriend. In place of the first course listings was the message: "Dear Vanessa, I love you so much I want to share my life with only you . . . and I am ready to prove it! Will you marry me? Always, Michael." How could she refuse?

Under the creative direction of the proprietors, George and Jenifer Lang, the Viennese-born chef, Thomas Ferlesch, has crafted country French cuisine for almost a decade. A master of such delicacies as Four-Way Salmon (tidbits of fish that are smoked, poached, marinated with dill, and à la tartare), *pot-au-feu,* and Provençal fish stew, the chef is also popular for his Sunday brunch. Who says romance happens only at night? This Sunday morning-after feast is filled with tempting treats that are simple to make. Skip the mimosas and whip up a pitcher of pear champagne instead. Jenifer Lang describes this drink, invented by her husband, as "fizzy soda for the nineties. It's sweet, without being too sweet." The Smoked Salmon Benedict, also invented by George, is a tasty alternative to traditional Eggs Benedict. Polish off your meal with a refreshing spoonful of your favorite berry sherbert. "The key is to be as relaxed and comfortable as possible" says Jenifer. If this doesn't set hearts aflutter, you can always try painting a nude nymph on your wall.

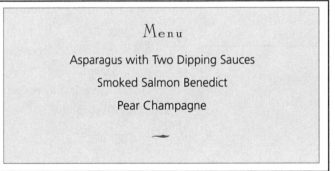

Menu

Asparagus with Two Dipping Sauces

Smoked Salmon Benedict

Pear Champagne

Asparagus with Two Dipping Sauces

1 pound fresh asparagus, peeled
  (see page 11)
About ½ cup unsalted butter

2 large eggs
Coarse salt and freshly ground black
  pepper

Presentation is the key to this recipe. Use a platter large enough to hold everything: the asparagus and the soft-boiled eggs and the brown butter that are the "dipping sauces." Served on a silver tray, this dish makes an ideal romantic breakfast in bed.

1 FILL A large pot with water, add salt, set the pot over high heat, and bring to a boil. Add the asparagus and cook until the stalks are crunch tender but not soft when pricked with a fork, 3 to 4 minutes. Drop the asparagus into a bowl of cold water to stop the cooking process and drain well.

2 WHILE THE asparagus cooks, melt the butter in a small saucepan set over medium-high heat and cook until it is aromatic and nutty brown in color, 3 to 5 minutes. Watch, taking care not to burn the butter. Divide the butter between 2 ramekins and keep warm.

3 COOK THE eggs for 3 minutes in a small pot of boiling, salted water. Remove the eggs from the water and place in egg cups. Cut off the tops of the egg shells.

4 TO SERVE, arrange the asparagus in the center of a warm platter lined with a napkin. Set the eggs and ramekins of butter at each end. Serve at once with salt and pepper on the side. Dip the stalks into the eggs and the butter separately.

Smoked Salmon Benedict

For the Béarnaise sauce

1 tablespoon chopped fresh tarragon
 leaves, or ½ tablespoon dried
 tarragon
1½ tablespoons tarragon or white
 wine vinegar
1 tablespoon minced shallots
½ teaspoon freshly ground black
 pepper

⅔ cup dry white wine
3 large egg yolks
1 cup (2 sticks) unsalted butter, diced,
 at room temperature
Dash salt and cayenne pepper

Juice of 1 lemon, plus more for adjusting
 the flavor of the sauce
4 large eggs
2 English muffins, split

8 thin slices (approximately ¼ pound)
 smoked salmon
2 sprigs fresh tarragon, for garnish

1 TO MAKE the sauce, combine the tarragon, vinegar, shallots, pepper, and wine in a nonreactive medium saucepan. Set the pan over medium-high heat, bring the liquid to a boil, and cook until the mixture is reduced to ¼ cup of liquid, about 4 minutes. Remove from the heat and let cool.

2 IN A double boiler or bowl set over a pan of simmering water over medium heat, whisk the egg yolks together with 2 tablespoons water until lemony in color. Continue whisking over the water until the mixture is light and fluffy. Remove the pan from the heat and add the pieces of butter, one at a time, whisking each one in until it is completely incorporated. Strain the emulsion through a fine-mesh sieve into a small mixing bowl. Whisk in the cooled tarragon reduction and season with salt, cayenne pepper, and lemon juice to taste. Keep warm.   *continued*

> **Popular since**
>
> George invented it in 1975, this version includes smoked salmon instead of Canadian bacon.
>
> —

3 IN A saucepan over medium heat, add water to about 5 inches deep and the juice of 1 lemon (to help the eggs coagulate). Bring to a simmer. One at a time, break the eggs into the water, keeping them as separate as possible. Poach for 3 minutes.

4 TOAST THE English muffins until light brown. Place 2 slices of smoked salmon on each toasted muffin half and set two halves each on warm serving plates.

5 USING A slotted spoon, remove the eggs as soon as they are firm but not well done. Immediately set them on a linen napkin to remove the excess water. Trim off any ragged egg white. Place an egg on top of each muffin half. Coat each egg with some of the Béarnaise sauce and serve the remaining sauce on the side. Garnish with fresh tarragon and serve.

Pear Champagne

¼ cup sugar

1 slice fresh ginger, the size of a
  quarter

1 fresh, firm, ripe Bartlett, Anjou, or
  Comice pear, peeled and cored

About 1 tablespoon pear brandy

1 bottle dry champagne, cold

1 IN A small, deep saucepan set over high heat, combine 2 cups water with the sugar and ginger and bring to a boil. Stand the pear upright in the liquid, which should barely cover the pear. Reduce the heat and simmer until the pear is slightly crunchy yet almost cooked. (The cooking time will depend on the ripeness and variety of the pear.) Test with a toothpick inserted into the end of the pear. Remove from the heat and allow to cool in the syrup.

2 CUT THE pear lengthwise into quarters or sixths. Place one slice of pear upright in each of two champagne flutes. Pour about 1 teaspoon of pear brandy over each pear, fill the glasses with champagne, and serve at once.

Sarabeth Levine

Sarabeth's

New York

Scenario one: Wake up extra early on Sunday morning. Tiptoe downstairs to the kitchen and prepare a gorgeous plate of pumpkin waffles topped with sour cream and crunchy pumpkin seeds. Make a pitcher of four flowers juice, set the table, and wait for your special someone to make an appearance.

Scenario two: If the waffles are getting cold, pile everything on a breakfast tray and go back upstairs to surprise your honey in bed.

Either way, it's hard to go wrong with this morning glory food from Sarabeth Levine, the owner of the Sarabeth's cozy restaurants and bakeries in New York City. Manhattanites line up outside to feed their lovers the morning after-bedtime-story dishes such as Goldie Lox Scrambled Eggs and Mama Bear Porridge.

"There is something very special about the morning meal—brunch is a celebration," says Sarabeth, who has spent the past twenty years perfecting her recipes for this meal. "It's an art form. A chef uses food as a painter uses paint," she explains. "Think about what happens in baking. If you vary the flour, the butter, add a little more sugar here, a little yeast there, you can come out with a scone or a muffin or end up with a beautiful pastry."

She recalls an intimate rendezvous with a brioche. "I broke it open—it was still warm. I tore off a little piece and dipped it in a pot of butter. It was magnificent. The consistency was perfect. I thought I went to heaven. I can still close my eyes and recapture that moment."

According to Sarabeth, the texture of the food is what gives it its sensuality. She enjoys mixing different sensations together as she has done by garnishing soft fluffy waffles with crisp pumpkin seeds. Just don't ask her husband Bill to serve it to her in bed. "I hate all the crumbs," she says.

Menu

Pumpkin Waffles with Sour Cream and
Toasted Pumpkin Seeds

Four Flowers Juice

—

Pumpkin Waffles with Sour Cream and Toasted Pumpkin Seeds

⅔ cup pumpkin seeds

4 large eggs

¾ cup heavy cream

⅓ cup milk

⅓ cup unsweetened pumpkin purée

1 tablespoon unsalted butter, melted

3 cups sifted basic waffle mix
    (Bisquick)

3 tablespoons sugar

Scant ⅛ teaspoon cinnamon

Scant ⅛ teaspoon nutmeg

Scant ⅛ teaspoon ground ginger

About ⅓ cup clarified butter

Powdered sugar, for dusting

About ¾ cup sour cream

About ¼ cup golden raisins

4 perfect strawberries with stems, each
    dipped in honey

This breakfast treat, packed with the earthy flavor of pumpkin, is a delightful way to say good morning.

1 PREHEAT THE oven to 350°F. Spread the pumpkin seeds on a cookie sheet. Bake the seeds, shaking the pan often to toast evenly, until light brown, crisp, and aromatic, 10 to 15 minutes. Remove from the oven and reserve. Turn the oven temperature down to 300°F.

2 COMBINE THE eggs, cream, milk, and pumpkin purée. Add the butter and mix well. Stir in the waffle mix, sugar, cinnamon, nutmeg, and ginger. Mix well. This is a very thick batter.

3 HEAT A waffle iron and brush it with clarified butter. Following the manufacturer's directions, ladle ¼ to ⅓ cup of the batter in the center of the waffle iron, close the lid, and bake until done. Continue making waffles until the batter is finished. Place the cooked waffles on a cookie sheet in the oven to keep them warm until all the waffles are cooked.

4 TO SERVE, place 2 waffles on a warm dinner plate and dust with powdered sugar. Using an ice-cream scoop, center a half-globe of sour cream on top of each waffle. Surround the sour cream with a fistful of toasted pumpkin seeds and raisins. Top with 2 honey-dipped strawberries.

Four Flowers Juice

Nectar fit for the gods, this fruit-juice combination is as pretty to look at as it is refreshing to drink.

2 ripe bananas, peeled and cut into chunks
1 cup fresh orange juice
Quarter of a very ripe pineapple, peeled, cored, and cut into chunks
2 teaspoons fresh lemon juice
1 tablespoon grenadine
1 tablespoon maple syrup
¼ cup water
2 whole strawberries with stems

1 PURÉE THE banana chunks with a little orange juice in a blender or food processor. Transfer to a large pitcher. Purée the pineapple with a little orange juice and add to the banana purée.

2 WHISK THE two purées together, add the remaining orange juice, lemon juice, grenadine, maple syrup and water, mix well, and chill.

3 POUR THE juice into chilled glasses (set them in the freezer for a few minutes). Cut a slit in the pointed end of each strawberry, perch them on the edge of the glasses, and serve at once.

Wayne Nish

March restaurant

New York

DINING AT MARCH restaurant is like being on the set of a Merchant-Ivory production. The restaurant, in a turn-of-the-century town house, has floor-to-ceiling mirrors flanking a marble-topped Louis XV side table; botanical prints with ornate antique frames line the walls, and banquettes covered in luxurious fabrics set off a Lalique chandelier. A staircase in the rear of the restaurant descends to a garden patio that has ivied trellises and lush flowerbeds. This enchanted Eden is naturally the place for marriage proposals and they occur there on a regular basis. Less frequent is the discovery of a woman's undergarment on the banquette at the end of the evening, left by a playful, if forgetful, couple.

March has been called a "fantasy for all the senses." The same could be said for the chef and co-owner, Wayne Nish, the original tall, dark, and handsome man. Sitting by the window overlooking his enchanted garden, he considers romance and the art of seduction. "If I were interested in a woman enough that I would want to seduce her, then I would choose textures that were sensual—things that would immediately be construed as sending a message. I go to things that are surprising, elegant, and unrestrained." He doesn't believe in the power of aphrodisiacs, but does think that the mere suggestion of them is delightful. His taste in music leans toward rock and rhythm and blues. "If I want to impress her, I would not blast rock and roll. I would keep it silent so that I didn't have to compete with extraneous sounds." For Wayne, the most important part of this intimate feast is behind the scenes. "If the meal is prepared without a lot of trouble or delay, than I know that the evening will be a success."

Menu

Sashimi of *Hamachi*

Loin of Veal with Black Truffles
and Braised Autumnal Vegetables

French Châteauneuf-du-Pape—
Domaine du Beaucastel, 1986

Panna Cotta with Bittersweet Almond Cream

California late-harvest Sauvignon Blanc—
Kent Rasmussen Winery, North Coast, 1993

127

Sashimi of *Hamachi*

The blending of olive oil and soy sauce on the same plate seems to be the perfect embodiment of East-West food combinations. Buy the best ingredients you can find. *Hamachi,* also known as Japanese yellowtail tuna, is an excellent fish, but others can be substituted, including white king salmon, fluke, flounder, halibut, bluefin tuna, ahi, striped bass, or black sea bass.

⅓ pound fresh *hamachi*

2 tablespoons extra virgin olive oil

2 tablespoons Japanese soy sauce

1 tablespoon white sesame seeds, not toasted

2 tablespoons finely cut fresh chives

1 CUT THE fish into very thin slices and arrange them evenly on two dinner plates.

2 DRIZZLE THE fish first with the olive oil, then with the soy sauce, and sprinkle on the sesame seeds and chives. Serve at once.

Loin of Veal with Black Truffles and Braised Autumnal Vegetables

For the vegetables

1 to 1½ tablespoons extra virgin olive
  oil
1 large shallot, sliced lengthwise
4 *cipollini*, or white pearl onions,
  peeled
2 tablespoons celery root diced into
  ¼-inch cubes
About 1 cup sliced assorted fresh wild
  mushrooms, such as trumpets,
  chanterelles, *enoki*, and shiitake
7 to 8 fingerling potatoes, scrubbed
  and cut into quarters
1 heaping tablespoon confit of garlic
  (page 11)
Sea salt

1 cup chicken stock
1 cup dry white vermouth
1 fresh black truffle, brushed clean of
  dirt
2 small Brussels sprouts, leaves
  separated and blanched for
  30 seconds
About 2 tablespoons chopped fresh
  chervil
About 2 tablespoons chopped fresh
  chives
About 2 tablespoons chopped fresh
  tarragon
1 tablespoon butter, or more to taste

Extra virgin olive oil
One 11-ounce loin of veal, trimmed
  of silverskin and fat
Sea salt

2 large cloves garlic, smashed
1 sprig fresh thyme, bruised
A few whole chervil leaves, for garnish

For this simple, well-balanced harvest dish, bite-size vegetables perfumed with fresh black truffle surround tender slices of veal.

1 FILM THE bottom of a small nonreactive saucepan with oil. Set the pot over high heat, add the shallot, and cook, stirring, for a few seconds. Add the onions, celery root, mushrooms, potatoes, confit of garlic, salt to taste, and chicken stock. Bring to a boil and cook uncovered until the veg- etables are nearly tender, 5 to 8 minutes. *continued*

2 TO COOK the veal, coat with oil the bottom of a medium skillet; set over high heat. Season the veal with salt and sear it until the meat is brown on all sides, about 5 to 8 minutes. Add the garlic and thyme. Continue cooking until the meat is firm to the touch, about 5 minutes longer. (An instant-read meat thermometer should read no more than 130°F for medium rare.) Remove the pan from the flame and let the meat rest in the pan on the back of the stove for at least 5 to 8 minutes, or until you finish cooking the vegetables.

3 WHILE THE veal cooks, check the vegetables. When the liquid is reduced to about 2 tablespoons, add the vermouth, bring to a boil, reduce the heat, and cook about 1 minute.

4 CUT THE truffle into paper-thin slices and add it, along with the Brussels sprout leaves and the herbs, to the vegetables. Cook until the vegetables are tender and the juices are reduced to a rich sauce, about 18 minutes for total cooking time. Swirl in the butter, taste, and correct the seasoning.

5 SPOON THE vegetables onto the side of a large warm dinner plate. Cut the veal into ¼-inch-thick slices and arrange on the other side of the plate, sprinkle a few whole chervil leaves on top, and drizzle a bit of the sauce on the edges of the meat. Serve at once.

Panna Cotta
with Bittersweet Almond Cream

For the panna cotta
¼ cup milk
1 package Knox unflavored gelatin
1¼ cups heavy cream
½ cup sugar

For the almond cream
⅓ cup sliced blanched almonds
¾ cup heavy cream
¼ cup sugar
Pinch salt
Almond essence to taste, or ⅛
    teaspoon pure almond extract

Pinch salt
1 cup sheep's milk yogurt or plain
    nonfat yogurt

2 sprigs fresh mint, for garnish
1 pint fresh raspberries or blueberries,
    for an optional accompaniment

The remarkable almond cream–dressed *panna cotta* at March is made with sheep's milk yogurt. Plain nonfat yogurt is a good substitute. Note that the *panna cotta* needs to be refrigerated for 24 hours before serving.

1 POUR THE milk into a glass measuring cup, whisk in the gelatin, and set the mixture aside to soften, about 5 minutes. Meanwhile, fill a saucepan with 2 to 3 inches of water and bring to a simmer. Remove from the heat. When the gelatin is soft, place the cup into the pan of hot water until the mixture becomes liquid, then stir until the gelatin is completely dissolved, about 5 minutes longer.

2 WHISK TOGETHER the cream, sugar, salt, and yogurt in a small saucepan set over moderately high heat. Heat the mixture gently until the sugar is completely dissolved. Remove from the heat and let cool slightly. Whisk in the dissolved gelatin and pass the mixture through a fine-mesh strainer.

continued

3 HAVE ON hand six ½-cup custard cups or ramekins set on a tray. Pour the custard into the cups or ramekins, cover with plastic wrap, and refrigerate for at least 24 hours.

4 TO PREPARE the almond cream, blend the almonds to a powder in a blender or food processor.

5 COMBINE THE cream, sugar, and salt. Bring to a simmer over moderate heat, remove the pan from the heat, and stir in the powdered almonds. Let the mixture cool to room temperature, about 2 hours. Pass the cream through a fine-mesh strainer. Whisk in the almond essence to taste. Can be stored, covered, and refrigerated.

6 TO SERVE, run a thin knife around the edge of each *panna cotta* and unmold onto rimmed, pretty dessert plates. Pour a generous amount of the almond cream over the *panna cotta,* allowing it to pool around the mold, and garnish with a sprig of mint. Or accompany the *panna cotta* with berries and serve the almond cream in a pitcher.

PATRONS COMING THROUGH the turnstile doors of Boulevard barely have time to catch their breath before being transported to the Belle Epoque fantasy inside. They cross a dazzling peacock mosaic at the entranceway, passing Art Nouveau–inspired glass light fixtures, twisted railings, and trompe l'oeil murals. Some take seats by the counter to enjoy the show in the open kitchen; others settle at the tables to enjoy views of the Bay.

The real gems are found in Nancy Oakes's kitchen. Mixing classic French with Asian, Mediterranean, and Latin ingredients, the chef creates New American treasures such as spit-roasted, cider-cured pork loin with grilled figs and grilled Hawaiian escolar. Customers satisfy a sweet tooth with vanilla bean crème brûlée or lemon buttermilk pie with blackberries in vanilla sugar that is served with whipped cream and blackberry sauce. Oakes recalls one woman so engrossed in her dessert that she didn't even notice the engagement ring at the bottom of her glass of champagne.

If you want to get your lover's attention, try making some of Nancy's favorite recipes: smoked salmon with caviar and pancakes and wild boysenberry shortcake. Packed with aphrodisiacs, this light menu is perfect for popping the question. "The reason I chose this dessert is that boysenberries are the most luscious of all berries, making them the most romantic," says Oakes. "Boysenberries are round and robust and burst open in your mouth!"

Although Nancy works in opulent surroundings at Boulevard, she would scale down the setting. "Serve this meal at your coffee table in front of the fireplace and just eat with your hands."

Nancy Oakes

Boulevard Restaurant

San Francisco, California

Menu

Smoked Salmon with Osetra Caviar
and Cottage Cheese Pancakes

Champagne—Bollinger, Spécial Cuvée, NV

Just-Baked Wild Boysenberry Shortcake

California late-harvest Sémillon—Far Niente, Dolce, 1994

⚊

Smoked Salmon with Osetra Caviar and Cottage Cheese Pancakes

Pairing smoked salmon with caviar is as old as Escoffier himself. But topping the slices with tiny cottage cheese and chive pancakes is as fresh as budding romance. Nancy prefers Summer Hill Smoked Salmon and flavorful organic clabbered cottage cheese from the Cowgirl Creamery. Large-curd cottage cheese is a good substitute.

—

For the pancakes

2 large eggs

8 chives, snipped

7 tablespoons large-curd cottage cheese, preferably clabbered organic

2 tablespoons all-purpose flour

¼ teaspoon sugar

2 pinches salt

4 very thin slices smoked salmon

1 tablespoon unsalted butter, softened

½ ounce osetra caviar

3 tablespoons Crème Fraîche (see page 15)

Fresh chives, snipped, for garnish

Freshly ground black pepper

1 PREHEAT THE oven to 300°F. Whisk the eggs and stir in the chives. Beat in the cottage cheese and then the flour, sugar, and salt.

2 HEAT A small skillet over medium-high heat. Coat the bottom of the pan with a film of olive oil. Ladle about ¼ cup batter into the skillet. When the pancake starts to turn light brown around edges, flip it and continue cooking until it is done, about 1 minute longer. Transfer to a baking sheet and keep warm in the oven while cooking the next pancakes.

3 PLACE 2 slices of smoked salmon on each serving plate. Lightly butter the pancakes and top each with about 1 teaspoon of caviar. Set the pancakes on top of the smoked salmon and then drizzle with crème fraîche. Sprinkle with snipped chives and freshly ground black pepper.

Just-Baked Wild Boysenberry Shortcake

For the shortcakes

2 cups self-rising flour

1 teaspoon salt

⅓ cup sugar, plus ¼ cup for dipping

1 to 1½ cups heavy cream

½ cup melted butter, cooled

For the topping

1 pint fresh wild boysenberries, washed and well drained

1 teaspoon fresh lemon juice

2 tablespoons Simple Syrup (see page 19), or more to taste

1 to 2 cups Whipped Cream (see page 14)

1 PREHEAT THE oven to 425°F. Stir the flour, salt and ⅓ cup sugar together. Stir in 1 cup of the cream, adding more if the dough seems dry. Using your hands, gather the dough together. When it holds together but is not sticky, turn onto a lightly floured flat baking sheet and pat into a square 2 inches high.

2 WITH A 4-inch round cookie cutter, cut the large square into 6 biscuits. Pour the melted butter into a soup dish and, in another soup dish, place about ¼ cup sugar. Dip each biscuit first into melted butter and then into sugar, coating it completely. Place the biscuits on another ungreased cookie sheet and bake until golden brown, 15 to 20 minutes.

3 CRUSH HALF of the berries with the lemon juice and mix with 1 to 2 tablespoons of simple syrup. Add the remaining berries and toss with a little more simple syrup, according to taste. Set aside.

4 SLICE THE warm shortcakes in half and spoon berries over the bottom halves. Cover with the top halves of the shortcake and pile on the whipped cream. Serve at once.

This recipe makes enough shortcakes for 6 people, so you and your sweetie will have enough for seconds and breakfast too! If you can't find fresh boysenberries, substitute blueberries, raspberries, or strawberries, adjusting the quantity of simple syrup to the sweetness of the berries.

Having trouble in the love department? Here's a quick remedy: Dinner for two at Aureole. You certainly won't have to call us in the morning. Described as "one of the best shows in town," Charlie Palmer's award-winning restaurant is a feast for the eyes and the tummy. Swing your date by the glass-fronted brownstone for a peek inside at the towering flower arrangements and scenes of foliage and animals sculptured in sandstone on the walls. Once inside, you'll be treated to a sneak preview from the kitchen before the main event of signature dishes such as sea scallop sandwich, grilled lobster, and roasted guinea hens. You may want to try one of Palmer's home-grown cheeses—they come from Egg Farm, a dairy that he established. Then sample one of his dramatic desserts that resemble "scale models for futuristic fountains."

Despite Charlie's reputation for generous portions at his restaurants, he believes in keeping things relatively light for romantic dinners at home. "It isn't Thanksgiving," he jokes, urging you not to overstuff your loved one. The other reason is time. "You don't want to be yelling, 'How's the wine?' from the kitchen because you aren't finished cooking."

How do chefs have any time to prepare home-cooked romantic meals? They don't. "When you are a chef, you have to do your courting from the restaurant," which is what he did in order to woo his wife, Lisa. Late-night dinners of caviar and toast, dining side by side at some out-of-the-way bistro, long walks on the beach and, yes, loads of time spent with their children are the keys to this couple's marital bliss. "It takes a special woman to put up with all of the late nights at the restaurant," Charlie says about his bride. "She must love me dearly."

Menu

Chilled Snap Pea Soup

Chicken Breast with Citrus-Tarragon Sauce
and *Haricots Verts*

Sauvignon Blanc

Chocolate Chocolate–Chip Cookie Napoleons

Chilled Snap Pea Soup

1 large carrot, trimmed and peeled

⅛ teaspoon saffron threads

2 cups vegetable stock

½ pound snap peas, blanched in
    boiling water for 1 minute

2 tablespoons minced scallions
    (whites only)

2 tablespoons minced celery

1 teaspoon minced fresh oregano

Coarse salt and white pepper

¼ cup plain yogurt, nonfat or regular

2 sprigs fresh oregano

1 AT LEAST 4 hours before you plan to serve, cut the largest part of the carrot crosswise into six ½-inch-thick discs of equal size. In a small saucepan over high heat, place 1 cup of water and the saffron and bring to a boil. Add the carrots, return to a boil, and immediately remove from the heat. Allow to cool. The carrots should be just tender and well flavored with saffron. Drain and pat dry. Cover with plastic and refrigerate until ready to use.

2 IN A medium saucepan over high heat, bring the vegetable stock to a boil. Reserve 6 blanched snap peas for garnish and refrigerate them. Add the remaining peas to the simmering stock along with the scallions, celery, minced oregano and salt and white pepper. Return to a boil. Immediately reduce the heat and simmer for 3 minutes. Let cool for 10 minutes before processing.

3 POUR THE soup into a food processor or a blender and process until smooth. Transfer to a nonreactive container and place in an ice-water bath to cool quickly. Cover and refrigerate for at least 4 hours or until well chilled.

4 WHEN THE soup is cold, whisk in the yogurt. Taste and adjust the seasoning with salt and white pepper. Serve in chilled flat soup bowls. Float 3 carrot discs and 3 snap pea pods on top of each serving. Garnish with a fresh oregano sprig and serve at once.

The freshness of this soup is a sweet surprise. Made creamy with yogurt, its tang and color aren't weighted down with any cream. A delightful prelude for sensations that follow.

Chicken Breast with Citrus-Tarragon Sauce and *Haricots Verts*

2 large oranges, peeled and sectioned (page 12), juice reserved
1 teaspoon fresh lemon juice
2 teaspoons olive oil
1 whole boneless, skinless chicken breast, split
Coarse salt and freshly ground pepper

1 teaspoon canola oil
1 teaspoon freshly grated orange zest
1 teaspoon minced fresh tarragon
½ pound *haricots verts,* trimmed and blanched in boiling water for 1 minute

1 COMBINE THE orange sections, orange and lemon juice, and the olive oil in a blender or food processor. Process until smooth and set aside.

2 WITH THE flat side of a meat cleaver or a large knife, pound each chicken breast half to flatten it slightly; season with salt and pepper to taste. Coat with oil the bottom of a medium nonstick sauté pan; set over medium-high heat. Sear the chicken breast until light brown, about 2 minutes; turn and sear the other side. Continue cooking, turning from time to time, until the chicken is cooked through, about 10 minutes. Transfer the chicken to a warm plate. Tent with aluminum foil and keep warm.

3 IN THE same sauté pan over high heat, add the reserved citrus mixture. Cook, stirring constantly, until the mixture has reduced to about ½ cup, about 5 minutes. Stir in the orange zest and tarragon. Add salt and pepper to taste.

4 IN A medium sauté pan over medium-high heat, toss the green beans with 1 tablespoon of the citrus sauce. Cook until just heated through, about 30 seconds.

5 MOUND SERVINGS of green beans on warm dinner plates. Top the beans with a chicken breast, spoon a portion of the reduced citrus sauce over, and serve.

Chocolate Chocolate—Chip Cookie Napoleons

For the cookies

6 ounces (¾ cup) chocolate chips, slightly chopped

6 tablespoons unsalted butter, at room temperature

¼ cup granulated sugar

3 tablespoons light brown sugar

1 tablespoon light corn syrup

1 tablespoon heavy cream

1 teaspoon pure vanilla extract

¾ cup all-purpose flour

½ teaspoon salt

½ teaspoon baking soda

1 pint good-quality ice cream (vanilla, coffee, or chocolate)

1 cup Chocolate Sauce, warm (see page 17)

1 PREHEAT THE oven to 350°F. Spray a flat baking sheet with nonstick cooking spray and set aside.

2 IN A food processor, pulse the chocolate chips 6 to 8 times. Transfer to a bowl. In the unwashed processor, process the butter, sugars, and corn syrup until creamy. Add the cream and vanilla and process until mixed. Add the flour, salt, and baking soda and process until combined. Add the chocolate chips and pulse 2 or 3 times.

3 DROP LEVEL tablespoons of batter about 3 inches apart onto the prepared sheet. Using your fingers, flatten the dough to a 2-inch round. Bake until the edges just begin to brown, about 12 minutes. Remove from the oven and let the cookies cool on the pan. Carefully transfer the cookies to a rack to cool completely. Store in an airtight container.

4 ABOUT 3 hours before serving, line a cake pan or small cookie sheet with plastic wrap. Soften the ice cream.

5 PLACE 2 cookies on the pan. Top each cookie with a scoop of ice cream. Press another cookie on top of the ice cream, spreading it out to the

Here's our version of an architectural dessert that might rival one of Charlie Palmer's masterpieces. If you'd rather not construct it from scratch, this dessert can be assembled with 6 thin, crisp bake-shop chocolate-chip cookies, your favorite store-bought ice cream, and a jar of Charlie Palmer's Chocolate Sauce.

edge. Add another layer of ice cream, top with a third cookie, and freeze until firm.

6 ABOUT 5 minutes before serving, set the napoleons on dessert plates. Heat the chocolate sauce over a pan of simmering water. Dip a table fork into the chocolate and paint squiggles of hot sauce over the plate. Serve at once.

"IT'S IMPORTANT TO have someone make you coffee in the morning . . . coffee beans are aphrodisiacs," says Cindy Pawlcyn, whose husband, Murdo Laird, has brought her coffee in bed for more than ten years. In exchange, Cindy cooks him dinner. "[He likes] nothing green and nothing on the bone," she says. Although her husband refuses to branch out beyond steak or chicken, Cindy has been known to sneak a pheasant or two by him.

The couple met after Cindy spotted him in the bar of her restaurant, Mustards Grill. She invited him to her house for a jeans and T-shirt dinner of steak and mushrooms Madeira. Eating every morsel, Murdo waited until after they were married to confess that he in fact hated mushrooms.

Cindy pleases all kinds of eaters at Mustards. Honeymooners and locals alike dine on smoked meats and mesquite-grilled fish with homemade relishes and sip wines from local vineyards. In season the property's vegetable gardens are filled with tomatoes, green beans, peas, and pumpkins, providing diners with fresh salads and side dishes. Blanketed in a golden sea of wild mustard in the spring, the roadside restaurant is a satisfying pit stop for travelers weaving their way through the wine estates along Napa Valley's Highway 29.

Nothing says "I love you" louder than a trip to the wine country. But if you can't get away, you can always wine and dine your loved one at home. The romantic recipes from the kitchen at Mustards Grill can be paired with a California Merlot or a bright Zinfandel. Chef Pawlcyn particularly likes the Zinfandel produced by Red and Green, a winery in Napa Valley. For less dexterous cooks, Cindy suggests sharing the cooking responsibility. That way," she laughs, "you can share the blame!"

Cindy Pawlcyn

Mustards Grill

Napa, California

Menu

Marinated Rock Cornish Game Hens with Red Wine Sauce

Grilled Yams and Potatoes with Moroccan Spices

Merlot

Your favorite chocolate torte

Espresso

⌐

Marinated Rock Cornish Game Hens with Red Wine Sauce

2 rock Cornish game hens

For the marinade

1 serrano chile, roasted and minced

2 cloves garlic, minced

¼ bunch cilantro, minced

2 tablespoons red wine vinegar

¼ cup Dijon mustard

¼ cup olive oil

¼ cup honey

Salt and white pepper

2 sprigs fresh cilantro, for garnish

For the sauce

1½ tablespoons butter

5 shallots, roughly chopped

1 bunch fresh thyme, or 1 tablespoon dried thyme

5 whole black peppercorns

1 cup full-bodied red wine

2 cups chicken stock

1 THE DAY before you plan to serve, rinse the game hens thoroughly under cold running water. Pat them dry with paper towels. Using poultry shears, cut up one side of the backbone. Lay the hen out on a board and flatten with the side of a meat cleaver or heavy skillet. Fold the wing tips back under the wings to secure them and place the birds in a nonreactive dish.

2 WHISK THE chile, garlic, cilantro, vinegar, mustard, oil, and honey together. Season to taste with salt and white pepper. Pour over the hens. Cover with plastic and marinate in the refrigerator for at least 24 hours before grilling.

3 TO MAKE the sauce, melt the butter in a heavy nonreactive saucepan over medium heat. Cook the shallots, stirring, until golden, about 6 minutes. Add the thyme and peppercorns. Cook, stirring, until aromatic, about 2 minutes. Add the wine and cook until it is reduced by two-thirds, about 8 minutes. Add the stock and reduce by half, about 15 minutes. Pass the mixture through a fine-mesh strainer set over a clean bowl. Taste and correct the seasonings. Cover until ready to serve. Heat to a simmer before using.

4 PREHEAT THE grill until the coals are white hot. Remove the hens from the marinade and discard the marinade. Place the hens, skin-side down, on the grill and sear until brown and crisp, 3 to 4 minutes; turn and cook, until brown, 3 to 4 minutes longer. Move the birds to a less hot area of the grill to continue cooking, turning a few times until the juices in the legs run clear when pierced with a fork, or until the desired doneness, about 20 minutes total cooking time. Remove from the grill and let rest for 5 minutes before serving.

5 LADLE A pool of red wine sauce onto each large warm dinner plate, place a hen in the center, and garnish with a sprig of fresh cilantro. Accompany with Grilled Yams and Potatoes with Moroccan Spices (recipe follows) and pass the sauce at the table.

Grilled Yams and Potatoes with Moroccan Spices

For harissa

2 ounces whole dried *arbol* chiles

2 ounces whole dried *ancho* chiles

3 large cloves garlic

1 tablespoon caraway seeds

For the vinaigrette

½ cup fresh lemon juice

2 shallots, minced

Pinch salt and freshly ground black pepper

1½ cups extra virgin olive oil

2 tablespoons olive oil

Salt and freshly ground black pepper

2 tablespoons Crème Fraîche (see page 15)

2 medium whole, unpeeled Yukon Gold potatoes, scrubbed and scored

2 medium whole, unpeeled yams, scrubbed and scored

About 1 teaspoon each chopped parsley, cilantro, and scallion, for garnish

1 FOR THE *harissa,* discard the stems and seeds and soak the chiles in boiling water for 1 hour; drain very well. Chop the chiles along with the garlic and caraway seeds. Crush in a mortar and pestle until the mixture becomes a paste. Press through a sieve, transfer to a small jar, and reserve. Keeps refrigerated for several weeks.

2 FOR THE vinaigrette, whisk together the lemon juice, shallots, and salt and pepper. Slowly whisk in the olive oil to emulsify. Stir in 2 tablespoons of *harissa.*

3 PREHEAT THE oven to 375°F. On a baking sheet, roast the potatoes and yams until tender, 35 to 45 minutes. Let cool.

4 Cut the potatoes and yams on the diagonal into ½-inch-thick slices. Brush the slices lightly with olive oil and season with salt and pepper. Grill on both sides until brown on the edges, about 2 minutes each side.

5 Serve with the game hens, placing 3 yam and 3 potato slices on each plate. Drizzle 2 teaspoons of the vinaigrette over. Top with a dollop of crème fraîche and sprinkle with chopped parsley, cilantro, and scallion.

Wʜᴇɴ Aʟᴇxᴀɴᴅʀᴀ Pᴀʏᴀʀᴅ has a craving, she walks past the mahogany-framed pâtisserie cases showing off exquisite petits fours, jewel-toned fruit tarts, and tea cakes baked by her husband, the pastry chef, François Payard. She ignores his rendition of the Louvre, a chocolate and hazelnut dome, and his signature Manhattan Tower, a seven-inch layering of chocolate mousse, chantilly, and crème brûlée, and heads straight to the kitchen for a bite of warm chicken salad. "She is my worst customer," laughs François, "and my mother-in-law is my best!"

What a shame! Especially when her husband is a third-generation, world-class French pastry chef. Fair-haired François met his wife six years ago at a trendy bar in Manhattan. They knew they were destined for each other after surviving a dinner date that lasted five hours. "We were at a restaurant which shall remain nameless and the service was very slow," says François. "I was getting impatient. It was very nerve-racking. Luckily, we had a lot to talk about."

When François proposed to Alexandra, the ring was concealed inside a box made out of chocolate—naturally. She left her job in advertising to help run their bistro soon after their engagement. "I'm glad we work together," says Alexandra. "Otherwise we would never see each other."

Occasionally, the couple does take a break, and Alexandra has even baked for François. On St. Valentine's Day, she surprised him with a Sacher torte that took her five painstaking hours to make. "I was not very impressed with the dessert, but . . . " François says.

"What?" Alexandra interrupts.

"No! No! Let me finish," he continues. "I loved that you were willing to spend all that time making me a present . . . that was the real gift."

Mᴇɴᴜ

Smoked Trout Salad with Lentils and Frisée

Chalone Chardonnay
Monterey, California, 1996

Lemon Tartlets

Smoked Trout Salad
with Lentils and Frisée

For the lentils

2 ounces bacon, lightly smoked

1 medium onion, cut into ¼-inch dice

1 small carrot, cut into ¼-inch dice

1 small turnip, cut into ¼-inch dice

1 celery stalk, cut into ¼-inch dice

10 ounces green lentils

Chicken stock, to cover vegetables

1 sprig thyme

1 sprig rosemary

1 clove garlic

5 sprigs parsley

Salt

For the mustard dressing

1 teaspoon Dijon mustard

3 tablespoons red wine vinegar

½ cup plus 1½ tablespoons grape seed
   oil or olive oil

Coarse salt and freshly ground black
   pepper

To serve

1 smoked brook trout, about 1 pound,
   cut into fillets (available in fish
   specialty stores)

2 small heads California frisée

Sprig cervil, for garnish

> A delightful and satisfying entrée with intriguing contrasts of temperature and flavor: beginning with a base of warm herb-scented lentils, enhanced by cold smoked trout, and finished with mustard-dressed spiky frisée.

1 TO PREPARE the lentils, cook the bacon in a skillet over medium heat until it gives up its fat, about 3 minutes. Add the diced vegetables and cook, stirring, until softened, about 5 minutes. Add the lentils and cook for 2 minutes. Add enough chicken stock to cover the vegetables. Add the thyme, rosemary, garlic, and parsley and cover the pan. Bring to a boil, reduce the heat, and simmer until the lentils are *al dente*, about 15 minutes. Season with salt and cook until the liquid is evaporated, about 5 minutes longer. Remove from the heat and cool to room temperature. Can be done ahead—store covered in the refrigerator.

2 To PREPARE the dressing, in a small bowl, whisk the mustard, vinegar, and oil together until it becomes an emulsion. Season with salt and pepper to taste. Cover and set aside.

3 IF THE lentils are cold, warm them a bit and stir in 2 to 3 tablespoons of dressing. Place a 3-inch ring mold or cookie cutter in the center of a dinner plate and pack it with lentils. Remove the mold. Cut the trout fillet in half and top the lentils with the trout.

4 IN A separate bowl, dress the frisée with the mustard dressing and toss until coated. Finish the plate by mounding the frisée on top of the trout. Add a sprig of chervil on the side for garnish and serve at once.

Lemon Tartlets

For the pastry

¼ cup (½ stick) unsalted butter,
    at room temperature
½ cup powdered sugar

¾ cup plus 1½ tablespoons flour
Pinch salt
1 medium egg

For the filling

2 large lemons, 1 zested and juiced,
    the other reserved for garnish
1 large egg
¼ cup sugar

1 tablespoon unsalted butter, cubed
Mint leaves, for garnish
Apricot Glaze (see page 18)

Delicate tartlets filled with pale yellow citrus cream provide an elegant finish to a meal.

1 PREPARE THE pastry at least 6 hours in advance. Cream the butter in a food processor until smooth. Sift together the sugar, flour, and salt, add the mixture to the butter, and process for a few pulses. Add the egg and process until the dough forms a ball, but do not overmix. Wrap the dough in a sheet of plastic and chill for at least 2 hours.

2 ROLL OUT the dough on a floured work surface to a circle ⅛ inch thick. Cut out four rounds of dough each about 6 inches across with a pastry wheel. Grease the bottoms of four tart molds (4 inches in diameter by 1½ inches deep) with removable bottoms. Press the dough into the tart molds and firmly up the sides. Trim off excess dough, prick the dough carefully with a fork, and freeze for 1 hour.

3 WHEN READY to bake, preheat the oven to 325°F. Set the tart shells on a baking sheet and bake for 10 minutes, rotating the tray after 5 minutes. The crusts should have little or no color. Cool on a rack. Leave the oven on.

4 TO PREPARE the filling, whisk together the lemon juice, zest, egg, sugar, and butter in a metal mixing bowl set over a pan half full of barely simmering water. When the butter has melted and the mixture is homogeneous, remove the bowl from the heat and let the mixture cool. Pour the filling into the tart shells and bake until the center of the lemon filling has set, about 8 minutes. Cool on a rack.

5 WITH A zester, cut lengthwise grooves in the rind of the second lemon. Cut 4 paper-thin slices from the center. Remove any seeds from the slices and place one slice in the middle of each tart. Decorate with mint leaves and then glaze with warm apricot glaze. Set the tarts aside unrefrigerated for at least 1 hour and serve them at room temperature.

AN ORDER OF veal kidneys changed Carole Peck's life. A number of years ago, a mutual friend invited her and a French artist, Bernard Cabernet-Jarrier, to dinner. "I was twenty-two at the time," she says. "He must have been impressed that someone so young and American could have sophisticated taste." After sampling the veal kidneys, they agreed that they were not cooked to perfection and fell into a lengthy discussion about the proper cooking technique.

A short while later, Carole invited Bernard to her home in Connecticut. She served roasted calf's liver. A few nibbles and he was hooked. Bernard moved in the following month. "I was sort of between boyfriends at the time, so I thought let's try it out," Carole teases. Good thing she did.

With the exception of a few marital spats ("who doesn't?"), Carole and Bernard share a lovely life together. In addition to running The Good News Café, the talented chef and her husband enjoy local trips to flea markets, where they add to their collections of vintage stemware and miniature stoves. "We are big antiquers," says Carole. "We can pick out the exact same thing without saying anything to each other." Most important, it is their taste in good food that has kept this marriage going. "Bernard says that if I were a hamburger girl, this never would have worked."

What does Chef Peck think about bringing a date home for dinner? "I think it's a great idea. It's a way to show him what your tastes are, and how you live, that you are not just a microwave baby. For me, eating is the foreplay to what is going to happen next." To enhance your romance, use Carole's secret ingredient: ginger. "I could have it on everything," she raves. "It warms the whole body and gets you so excited that you might as well continue!"

Menu

Caviar with Blini or Toast

Champagne—Veuve Clicquot-Ponsardin

Lamb Meatballs with Curried Angel Hair Pasta

California Cabernet Sauvignon—Swanson Vineyards, 1995

Scented Cherries and Marquis du Chocolat

California Muscat—Bonny Doon, Vin du Glacier

Lamb Meatballs

10 ounces ground lean lamb	¼ cup chopped cilantro
1 teaspoon chopped fresh chile, or ¼ teaspoon red pepper flakes	¼ cup chopped fresh mint
	2 teaspoons coarse salt
2 cloves garlic, minced	Freshly ground black pepper

1 MIX THE lamb together with the chile, garlic, cilantro, mint, salt, and pepper. Roll the mixture into 1½-inch-diameter balls. Place the meatballs in a shallow baking dish and refrigerate until set, about 1 hour.

2 PREHEAT THE oven to 425°F. Bake the meatballs until cooked, firm, and browned, about 10 minutes. Transfer to a warm dinner plate and serve with Curried Angel Hair Pasta (recipe follows).

Curried Angel Hair Pasta

24 baby green beans, washed, stem
    end removed, and blanched
    (page 10)
1 tablespoon coarse salt
¼ pound angel hair pasta
1 tablespoon curry powder

½ cup olive oil
10 medium fresh shiitake mushrooms,
    stemmed
12 basil leaves, cut in half
Juice of 1 large lime

1 COOK THE pasta in the water used for blanching the beans until it is *al dente,* about 5 minutes. Drain.

2 COMBINE THE curry powder and ¼ cup of the olive oil in a mixing bowl, add the drained pasta, and, using chopsticks, stir to separate and coat the pasta.

3 HEAT A wok or a large sauté pan over high heat, add the remaining ¼ cup oil, and, when it is smoking, cook the beans, stirring, for 1 minute. Add the mushrooms and cook, stirring, until they are softened, about 3 minutes. Add the basil and cook until it is wilted, about 1 minute. Toss in the curried pasta and lime juice and stir well.

As it is written, the recipe results in a dry tossed noodle dish. If you prefer things more saucy, reserve some of the water used to boil the pasta and stir a few tablespoons into the pasta right before you serve it.

Scented Cherries
and Marquis du Chocolat

For the cherries

½ pound fresh ripe cherries, washed
   and pitted

½ cup sugar

½ tablespoon grated fresh ginger

2 tablespoons water

For the Marquis

8 ounces bittersweet chocolate, cut
   into pieces

½ cup (1 stick) unsalted butter, cut
   into pieces

5 large eggs, separated

¼ cup flour, sifted

1 MIX THE cherries, ¼ cup of the sugar, and the ginger. Set aside for 30 minutes while the cherries give up some of their juices. Add the water and cook the cherries over medium heat until soft, about 15 minutes.

2 PREHEAT THE oven to 400°F. Butter and flour six ramekins. Melt the chocolate in a stainless mixing bowl set over simmering water. Remove the bowl from the heat, stir in the butter, and set the mixture aside.

3 BEAT THE egg whites until they form stiff peaks and set aside. Whisk the egg yolks until frothy, add the remaining ¼ cup sugar, and beat until the mixture is thick and a light lemon color, about 4 minutes. Mix in the flour.

4 FOLD THE egg yolk mixture into the chocolate. Quickly fold in the whites in 3 separate batches. Blend each addition in thoroughly so there are no white streaks.

5 POUR THE batter into the prepared ramekins. Bake for 15 minutes. Remove from the oven and immediately cover tightly with aluminum foil. Let the cakes steam for 15 minutes more, while resting on a cake rack. Remove the foil, turn the cakes out onto dessert plates, and serve with the warm cherries.

It's early afternoon, and Georges Perrier, wearing a warm-up suit, whisks around Le Bec Fin folding and refolding napkins. Like a general inspecting his troops, he checks every glass, knife, and fork. As one of the highest ranked culinary authorities, the French-born chef is driven to maintain his standards since he was inducted into the Maîtres Cuisiniers de France (the premier international society) in 1976 and earning the Silver Toque, the most coveted trophy in the world of haute cuisine.

A prime location for courtly love, Le Bec Fin, a modern-day Camelot, is a beautiful jewel tucked behind golden doors on Walnut Street. Seated on French period furniture in the Louis XVI style dining room that shimmers in crystal and silk, lords and ladies indulge in a six-course dinner. Servers lift silver domes in unison to reveal specialties such as *cailles farcies au foie gras* (quail stuffed with *foie gras*), *galette de crabe* (Perrier's signature crab cake), and *carré d'agneau au chutney, sauce au curry de Madras* (rack of baby New Zealand lamb with chutney and curry sauce). Surprisingly, most guests make it to dessert, elaborate cakes, tarts, and mousses brought on a triple-tiered cart. If this restaurant doesn't work, nothing will.

But at home, instead of an elaborate multicourse banquet, Perrier would choose simpler entrées with provocative ingredients. "When I cook at home, my approach is simple," says Perrier with a marked French accent. "I like to stay much more conservative. For example, I would cook lamb or fish instead of pigeon—something I know my date would like." He would begin the evening with caviar. A delicate Dover sole prepared with two sauces would follow and, for dessert, chocolate mousse—"without a doubt, I would not move from my *chocolat!*"

Menu

Osetra Caviar

Champagne

Grilled Dover Sole with Golden Pepper Coulis and Parsley Essence

White Burgundy, Pouligny from Sauget

Dark Chocolate Mousse

—

Grilled Dover Sole with Golden Pepper Coulis and Parsley Essence

Two sauces, one of sweet yellow peppers, the other an essence of parsley, add sparkle and pizzaz to the Dover sole, considered the king of fish.

For the coulis

1 medium yellow bell pepper, roasted, peeled, and seeded (page 12)

1 tablespoon rich chicken stock

1 tablespoon sherry vinegar

1 tablespoon olive oil

Salt and white pepper

For the essence

1 clove garlic, peeled

1 shallot, peeled

2 bunches flat-leaf (Italian) parsley, stems removed

¼ cup extra virgin olive oil

Salt and white pepper

1 tablespoon extra virgin olive oil

2 tablespoons chopped fresh *fines herbes*: tarragon, thyme, chives, and chervil

Salt and white pepper

4 fillets fresh Dover sole

½ pound fresh angel hair pasta

1 tablespoon unsalted butter

1 FOR THE coulis, puree the pepper, chicken stock and vinegar in a blender or food processor until smooth. With the machine running, add the olive oil and salt and pepper to taste. Transfer to a small dish, cover with plastic, and reserve at room temperature.

2 FOR THE parsley essence, preheat the oven to 400°F. Lightly oil the garlic and shallot, place them on a baking pan, and roast until brown, about 15 minutes. Remove from the oven and set aside. Blanch the parsley leaves in boiling salted water for 5 minutes. Drain and plunge in ice water to set the color. Drain well, shaking off any excess water. Puree the roasted garlic and shallot, parsley leaves, and olive oil until very smooth. Transfer to a bowl and season with salt and pepper to taste. Cover and reserve at room temperature.

3 TO PREPARE the fish, mix the olive oil, herbs, and salt and pepper together. Rub the mixture over the fillets and set them aside to marinate while heating the grill until the coals are white hot or preheating the broiler, about 10 minutes. Oil the grill. Sear the fillets on both sides until they are opaque but barely cooked, 3 to 4 minutes per side. Transfer to a warm plate and lightly tent with foil.

4 COOK THE pasta until *al dente*, 3 to 4 minutes. Drain and toss with butter.

5 TWIRL A nest of pasta in the center of each of two large dinner plates. Place one fillet on either side of the pasta. Place 2 tablespoons of each sauce on opposite sides of the plate. Serve at once.

Dark Chocolate Mousse

4½ ounces semisweet chocolate, chopped into pieces

7 tablespoons unsalted butter, cut into pieces

3 pasteurized eggs, separated

Pinch salt

2 tablespoons sugar

1 tablespoon strong, freshly brewed espresso

Whipped Cream (see page 14), for garnish (optional)

1 AT LEAST 2 or up to 24 hours before you plan to serve, melt the chocolate and butter in a metal mixing bowl set over simmering water, stirring until smooth. Remove the bowl from the heat, but keep the mixture warm.

2 IN A very clean, dry mixing bowl, beat the egg whites with a pinch of salt to soft peaks only. Transfer to another bowl. In another mixing bowl, beat the egg yolks until they are slightly frothy and slowly add the sugar; continue beating until the mixture forms light yellow ribbons.

3 WHISK THE egg yolk mixture and the espresso into the chocolate. Gently fold in the egg whites. Pour immediately into individual *pots de crème* or balloon-shaped wine glasses. Cover lightly with plastic and refrigerate for at least 2 hours. Present the mousses on pretty dessert plates and pass a bowl of whipped cream.

CANCER ALMOST KILLED Christina Pirello. Food and romance saved her life. Christina was just twenty-six years old when she was diagnosed with an acute form of leukemia—a terminal condition. She was determined to fight the disease without invasive chemotherapy. A friend told her about Robert Pirello, who ate an ultrahealthy diet—a macrobiotic one that could quite possibly cure her cancer.

Christina was already a vegetarian, but the notion that food could save her life seemed far-fetched. Desperate, she arranged a meeting.

After the first bite of her first macrobiotic meal—miso soup, rice salad, grilled tempeh, corn on the cob with *umeboshi* (salted plum) paste, and an assortment of seaweed—Christina remembers thinking, "Death would be better." Still Robert's passion was infectious. And what did she have to lose? For the next thirteen months, Robert taught his pupil the basics of macrobiotics. Her health and cooking abilities improved simultaneously. After a long and torturous struggle, and much to the surprise of her doctors, Christina ended up virtually cancer-free.

In addition to her recovering health, another wonderful thing was happening—love. Christina, a smiling redhead, remembers what happened the day they came back from a lecture. "We were standing in front of my apartment and he said, 'I've made a decision, I want to marry you and spend the rest of our lives together.'" Since then, Christina and her husband have been busy spreading the gospel of macrobiotics through their business, MacroChef, teaching, and writing. Now, Christina hosts her own television show, *Christina Cooks!*, on PBS.

Menu

Mushroom and Leek Strudel

Apricot-Mustard Tempeh on Brown Rice with Wilted Greens

California Sauvignon Blanc—Frey Vineyards (organic)

Suggested Dessert: Pecan Tarts with Chocolate Sauce

159

Mushroom and Leek Strudel

For the filling

Extra virgin olive oil

1 to 2 small leeks, split lengthwise, rinsed well, and finely sliced

Soy sauce

1 portobello mushroom, cleaned and thinly sliced

2 cups button mushrooms, cleaned and thinly sliced

Balsamic vinegar

For the pastry

2½ cups whole wheat pastry flour

⅛ teaspoon sea salt

2 teaspoons baking powder

½ teaspoon dried basil

¼ cup corn oil

⅔ cup unflavored rice milk or soy milk

1 TO PREPARE the filling, lightly coat with oil a medium nonreactive deep skillet; set over high heat, add the leeks and a splash of soy sauce, and cook, stirring, for 2 minutes. Stir in the mushrooms, add a bit more soy sauce, and cook, stirring, until the mushrooms begin to exude their juices. Sprinkle lightly with balsamic vinegar and continue to cook over low heat, stirring, until all liquid has been reabsorbed and the mushrooms are limp, about 15 minutes. Set aside to cool.

2 TO PREPARE the dough, combine the flour, salt, baking powder, and basil in a food processor. Add the corn oil and pulse 4 or 5 times, until the mixture has the texture of wet sand; do not overmix. Add the rice milk and pulse until the dough gathers itself into a moist, cohesive ball. Again, do not overmix.

3 PREHEAT THE oven to 350°F. Roll out the dough between two sheets of parchment paper into a rectangle about 9 by 13 inches and ⅛ inch thick.

Spread the cooled filling over the surface, leaving a 1-inch border exposed on the long side of the rectangle furthest from you. Roll up the dough and the filling, jelly-roll–style, to form a thick cylinder. Transfer the strudel to a parchment paper–lined baking sheet. Seal the ends of the strudel with a fork. With a sharp knife, make 6 to 8 slits in the top of the strudel to allow the steam to escape and to mark portions. Lightly brush the strudel with oil. Bake until the pastry is golden brown and the mushroom juices bubble through the slits, 30 to 45 minutes.

Apricot-Mustard Tempeh on Brown Rice with Wilted Greens

This tempeh will be sure to muster oohs and ahs from even the most loyal meat eater. The secret is the combination of flavors in the tangy sauce.

1 cup short-grain brown rice, well rinsed

2¼ cups spring or filtered water

Pinch sea salt

Safflower oil, for shallow frying

8 ounces tempeh, cut into 1-inch triangular pieces

1 red onion, sliced into thin half-moons

1 to 2 small turnips, sliced into thin half-moons

1 carrot, cut into fine matchsticks

Spring or filtered water

1 bunch broccoli rabe, cooked until tender and cut into bite-size pieces

1 lemon, zested and juiced

Small handful minced fresh parsley

For the sauce

½ cup unsweetened apricot jam

½ cup stone-ground mustard

2 teaspoons brown rice syrup

1 teaspoon soy sauce

½ teaspoon *umeboshi** vinegar

1 tablespoon balsamic vinegar

1 IN A large saucepan set over high heat, bring the rice, water, and salt to a boil. Reduce the heat to medium low, cover, and cook until the rice is tender and the liquid absorbed, about 1¼ hours.

2 TO PREPARE the tempeh, heat ½ inch safflower oil in a large, deep, nonreactive skillet with a lid. When the oil is hot, quickly fry the tempeh triangles until golden brown, about 2 minutes. Drain well on paper towels.

3 IN THE same skillet, over high heat, layer the onion, turnips, and carrot. Top with the fried tempeh and add a small amount of water, to come up about ⅛ inch on the sides of the pan. Cover and bring to a boil. Reduce the heat to low and cook for 5 to 7 minutes.

4 TO MAKE the sauce, mix the jam, mustard, syrup, soy sauce, and vinegars. Spoon the sauce evenly over the tempeh and vegetables. Cover and simmer for 10 minutes longer. Remove the cover and cook slowly until the sauce is reduced and thickens to a rich glaze, about 10 minutes longer.

5 JUST BEFORE serving, toss the broccoli rabe with the lemon juice and zest and arrange it in a ring around a mound of rice, spoon the tempeh and sauce over the rice, sprinkle with parsley, and serve at once.

Love Note: Umeboshi vinegar—a salty liquid left over from the pickling of *umeboshi* plums. Available in natural foods and specialty stores.

Nora Pouillon

Restaurant Nora

Asia Nora

Washington, D.C.

WHAT WITH ZIPPING back and forth between their two restaurants, Nora and Asia Nora, not to mention raising kids, it's a wonder that Nora Pouillon and her longtime love Steven Damato have any time for romance. But when Steven wants to plan a special evening at their home in Georgetown, he always makes sure that there is plenty of champagne and oysters around. "I love Tsar Nicoulai organic caviar . . . and Steven likes oysters, so I combine the two on the grill for a special appetizer. They are perfect to accompany the champagne that we buy from small boutique growers in France," Nora says with a slight Austrian accent.

In the garden at home, "Steven grows different varieties of lettuces especially for me, so we are able to pick fresh greens," Nora says. After they pick tomatoes, chervil, and nasturtiums from the garden, her daughter Nadia will cut them for the salad and pasta, while her other daughter, Nina, makes balsamic vinaigrette dressing. Nora cooks the pasta. Steven opens a bottle of organic wine. They'll have cold tomato salad with hot pasta and fresh mozzarella on top. Sometimes they'll eat poultry from the barbecue or an Asian-style duck, roasted in their wood-burning oven.

Her menu below is for an advanced cook. But you can make one recipe yourself and buy the rest. For beginners, she has this bit of advice: "Don't pick up a fancy cookbook and try to make something for the first time on the night of your date. Make something that you do well and dress it up—perhaps with a different garnish. Pay attention to detail but don't dash off to the kitchen every second."

Menu

Grilled Oysters with Cream and Caviar

French Chablis—René et Vincent Dauvissat, Vaillons, Premier Cru

Duck à l'Orange

California Zinfandel—Frog's Leap Winery, Napa Valley

Glazed Chocolate–Almond Cakes

Austria—Kracher, Beerenauslese, Grande Cuvée

Grilled Oysters with Cream and Caviar

6 tablespoons heavy cream

Juice of 1 lemon

Salt and freshly cracked pepper

1 dozen oysters, preferably small, cold-
water oysters from the Northwest

1 ounce caviar (possibly the American
brand, Tsar Nicoulai)

1 WHISK TOGETHER the cream and lemon juice and add salt and pepper to taste.

2 CAREFULLY SHUCK the oysters (see page 9), conserving the juices and keeping the oysters in their bottom shells. Top each oyster with 1 table-spoon of the cream mixture. Carefully place the oysters on the grill until they are warmed through, about 1 minute. Top with a spoonful of caviar and serve at once. Or, alternatively, arrange them on a cookie sheet that has been lined with crumpled aluminum foil or coarse salt to support the shells and bake in a 500°F oven for 1 minute. Top each oyster with a tablespoon of the cream mixture and a spoonful of iced caviar and serve at once.

This sublime combination, slightly salty, warm oysters tucked into lemon-scented cream and then topped with iced caviar, has all the makings of a very exciting evening.

Duck à l'Orange

1 duck, cut into serving-size pieces
1 to 1¼ cups orange marmalade
2 tablespoons soy sauce

2 tablespoons brandy or bourbon
Salt and freshly ground black pepper

1 PREHEAT THE oven to 350°F. Place the duck pieces, skin side up, in a baking pan that is large enough to hold the duck in one layer and bake for 12 minutes to release some of the fat. Remove the pan from the oven and pour off the fat.

2 WHISK TOGETHER the marmalade, soy sauce, brandy, salt, and pepper and paint the skin of the duck with the mixture. Return the duck to the oven. Basting the duck at least three times while it is cooking, roast until the pieces are crisp on the outside and the juices run clear when a thigh is pricked with a fork, about 1 hour. Let the duck rest for 5 minutes before transferring the pieces to warm dinner plates.

Glazed Chocolate—Almond Cakes

1⅓ ounces (about ¼ cup) semisweet
    chocolate, cut into small pieces
2 large eggs, separated
1⅓ ounces (about 2½ tablespoons)
    unsalted butter
¼ cup sugar

½ cup blanched slivered almonds,
    toasted (page 12) and
    chopped fine
¼ cup dried plain white bread crumbs
Rum-raisin ice cream
1 ounce milk chocolate shavings,
    for garnish

> The addition of ground almonds and dry bread crumbs gives these chocolate cakes a chewy nutty texture.

For the glaze

2 ounces semisweet chocolate, cut into
    small pieces

4 tablespoons unsalted butter,
    softened

1 PREHEAT THE oven to 325°F. Grease the inside of five or six 6-ounce aluminum cupcake molds with butter, dust with flour, and set aside on a baking sheet.

2 MELT THE chocolate in a metal bowl set over a pan of barely simmering water. Remove from the heat and cool.

3 BEAT THE egg whites until they begin to stiffen. In another bowl, beat the butter and sugar together until light and fluffy. Add the cooled chocolate and beat until the mixture is creamy, about 5 minutes. Add the egg yolks one at a time, beating well after each addition. Add the nuts and bread crumbs. Gently fold in the egg whites. Pour the batter into the prepared molds and smooth the tops.

4 BAKE UNTIL a toothpick inserted into the center comes out clean, about 30 minutes. Allow the cakes to cool in the molds for 10 minutes, remove and set them on a cake rack, and allow them to cool completely before glazing, about 1 hour.

continued

5 TO MAKE THE glaze, melt the chocolate in a metal bowl set over a pan of barely simmering water. Add the butter and stir until smooth. Remove from the heat and cool until it becomes the consistency of a thick cream, about 1 hour.

6 BRUSH THE cakes to remove loose crumbs and set them, still on the cooling rack, on a baking sheet to catch the drops. Slowly pour a pool of chocolate glaze onto the center of each cake. Using a long metal spatula, spread the glaze evenly over the top and sides of each cake. Allow to set about 2 hours at room temperature or 20 minutes in the refrigerator. To serve, set 1 glazed cake in the center of a pretty dessert plate, top with a scoop of rum-raisin ice cream, and decorate with chocolate shavings.

"I THINK WOMEN SHOULD ask out men more often," says the French-born chef Thierry Rautureau, whose wife invited him out to dinner almost twenty years ago. At Rover's, his contemporary French-fare bistro in Seattle, Thierry sets the scene in the country clapboard house with his seared sea bass, *foie gras* in chestnut purée, or smoked salmon flan decorated with blossoms of rosemary.

Once hearts are pounding, it's time for dinner at home. A feast filled with gems such as salmon, crème fraîche, lamb, cherries, and chocolate would certainly seal the deal. Rautureau has three rules for a successful evening: No animals, no children, and no neighbors; there should be no outside distractions. Thierry likes to preserve a peaceful and relaxing atmosphere to maintain the flow of conversation. Of course, once dessert is finished, you may no longer need to think of anything to say.

Thierry Rautureau

Rover's

Seattle, Washington

Menu

Smoked Salmon and Cucumber *Tians* with Crème Fraîche

French Cabernet Sauvignon—
Sancerre, Clos de la Crele, 1995

Loin of Lamb with Bing Cherry Sauce
and Nectarine Chutney

French Syrah—Hermitage, Jaboulet, 1990

Suggested dessert: Chocolate Tart
with Orange Crème Anglaise

169

Smoked Salmon and Cucumber *Tians* with Crème Fraîche

2 ounces smoked salmon, julienned

1 small shallot, minced

5 to 6 sprigs parsley, minced

6 to 8 chives, minced

½ tablespoon walnut or olive oil

3 tablespoons Crème Fraîche
   (see page 15)

Quarter of a cucumber, peeled and cut
   into small dice

1 small clove garlic, minced

Salt and freshly ground pepper

1 FOR THE salmon mixture, combine the salmon, ½ teaspoon minced shallot, ⅛ teaspoon each minced parsley and chives, oil, and 1 tablespoon of the crème fraîche. Taste and correct seasonings.

2 FOR THE cucumber mixture, combine ¼ cup of the cucumber, ½ teaspoon minced shallot, garlic, ½ teaspoon each minced parsley and chives, and 1 tablespoon of the crème fraîche. Taste and correct seasonings.

3 TO ASSEMBLE the *tians,* place a 3-inch round, straight-sided cookie cutter in the center of a serving plate and pack half of the cucumber mixture into the cutter. Top with half of the salmon mixture. With your fingers press down firmly onto the *tian*, so that it will keep its shape, and keep pressing down firmly while you remove the cookie-cutter mold. Repeat to make the second *tian,* top each with about ½ tablespoon crème fraîche, and serve at once.

Although this appetizer may look too elegant and taste too delicious to be simple, appearances can be deceiving. This pairing of salty salmon with herbs and crunchy cucumber is a snap to prepare.

Loin of Lamb with Bing Cherry Sauce and Nectarine Chutney

For the sauce

1 carrot, peeled and diced small

6 small shallots, chopped

1 garlic clove, chopped

2 tablespoons olive oil

5 sprigs thyme

3 bay leaves

3 cups good-quality beef stock

1 cup fresh Bing cherries, stemmed and pitted

2 lamb loins, about 8 ounces each, boned, silverskin removed, and patted dry with paper towels

Salt and freshly ground black pepper

¼ cup sugar

½ cup water

¼ cup raspberry wine vinegar

2 tablespoons butter, softened

For the chutney

1 red onion, chopped

4 nectarine halves, pits removed

¼ cup red wine vinegar

Sweet/tart cherries provide a rich sauce for the fragrant lamb and the accompanying nectarine chutney adds another dimension. (This chutney would also work well with a fish entrée.)

1 IN A large saucepan over medium-high heat, sauté the carrot, shallots, and garlic in the olive oil until light brown, about 5 minutes. Add the thyme, bay leaves, and beef stock and bring to a boil. Reduce the heat and simmer until the liquid is reduced by half, about 15 minutes. Strain through a fine-mesh strainer set over a bowl, wash out the saucepan, and return the sauce to the pan. Add the cherries, bring to a boil, reduce the heat, and simmer until the liquid is reduced by half, about 10 minutes longer. Set off the heat, but keep hot.

2 PREHEAT THE oven to 375°F. Sprinkle the meat with salt and pepper to taste. Sear the lamb loins on all sides in a sauté pan set over high heat. Place the meat in a roasting pan and finish cooking it in the oven for 3 to 4

minutes, until pink. Remove from the oven and let the meat rest for 5 minutes before cutting it into ½-inch-thick slices.

3 FOR THE raspberry caramel, combine the sugar and water in a medium nonreactive saucepan set over high heat. Stir until the sugar is dissolved, bring to a boil, and cook until the mixture caramelizes and is the color of a brown paper bag, 5 to 8 minutes. Watch carefully so it does not burn. Immediately remove from the heat and whisk in the raspberry vinegar. Add the raspberry caramel to the hot cherry sauce, stirring constantly. Taste and correct the flavors. Off the heat, swirl in the butter until it is melted.

4 TO MAKE the chutney, cook the onion with the nectarines and vinegar in a medium, nonreactive saucepan set over medium-low heat until the liquid has evaporated, about 5 minutes.

5 ARRANGE THE lamb slices in a circle in the center of a dinner plate. Ladle the sauce over the lamb. Garnish the plate with warm nectarine chutney and serve at once.

A BOY WONDER, Marcus Samuelsson is the chef's answer to the super-hero. Orphaned at the age of three in famine-ravaged Ethiopia, Marcus was adopted by a young couple in Sweden. There he discovered his passion for cooking. While other six-year-olds were playing with toys, Marcus was learning how to cook traditional Swedish food from his grandmother. At fourteen, he knew he wanted to be a chef and mapped out his career path accordingly. After cooking school, apprenticeships at both Aquavit and the famous Georges Blanc in Vonnas, France, and a couple of stints on a Norwegian cruise ship, Samuelsson became sous-chef at Aquavit and eventually took charge of the restaurant at the ripe old age of twenty-four.

Since then, Samuelsson, a long-limbed, long-lashed fellow with chisled features, has dazzled New Yorkers with his innovative twists on classic Scandinavian cuisine such as his signature herring taco and seared tuna with bay scallops washed down, of course, with the potato vodka known as aquavit. Like Superman's glacial palace, Aquavit is a mystical setting in which Marcus conjures up his culinary wizardry. At the bottom of a spiral stair, guests arrive at the bottom of a seven-story atrium in which a rainbow of kites hangs from the ceiling and a waterfall showers over a wall.

There is no steady Lois Lane in Samuelsson's life at the moment, so he is content to snuggle up to cookbooks at night, dreaming of the perfect strawberry soufflé. But if she were to put in an appearance, our hero would bring out an array of treats that only a three-star chef (and now you) could. "In a romantic meal, I always look for oysters, *foie gras,* strawberries, passion fruit, mango, champagne, and figs."

Menu

Champagne

Oysters Champagne

Salt-Cured Duck with Mango Risotto

Wild Strawberry Soufflés

Oysters Champagne

Kimchi, a Korean condiment of Napa cabbage pickled with chiles and vinegar, adds an unusual twist to the crunch of cucumbers and the kick of champagne to start off the evening.

—

1 tablespoon kimchi
½ small cucumber, peeled and halved
   lengthwise, and some seeds
   removed
4 fresh mint leaves
1 fresh basil leaf

6 oysters, fresh from the market
   (page 9)
¼ cup champagne
1 teaspoon finely minced shallot
Juice of half a lime

1 CHOP THE kimchi, cucumber, 2 of the mint leaves, and the basil together until very finely minced. Transfer to a bowl and reserve.

2 JUST BEFORE serving, shuck the oysters (see page 9). Divide the minced cucumber mixture between two martini glasses and place three oysters on top of the salad in each glass.

3 WHISK THE champagne, shallot, and lime juice together. Pour the mixture on top of the oysters and garnish with the remaining mint leaves.

Salt-Cured Duck

1½ cups kosher salt   2 whole duck breasts, with skin

1 COMBINE 2 quarts water with the salt in a deep, nonreactive bowl. Immerse the duck breasts in the brine, cover with plastic wrap, and weight down with a small plate on top of the plastic to keep the duck completely submerged. Set a large can or heavy jar on top of the plate if necessary. Refrigerate for 6 hours.

2 PREHEAT THE oven to 400°F. Remove the duck from the brine and pat dry with paper towels. Set a heavy iron skillet over medium-low heat, lay the duck breasts skin side down, and cook until the skin is crisp and browned, 12 to 15 minutes. Transfer the duck to a baking pan, again skin-side down, and bake in the oven until cooked to the desired doneness, 4 to 5 minutes for rare. Reserve the fat in the skillet for preparing the mango risotto.

3 TO SERVE, slice the duck breasts thinly on the diagonal and serve with Mango Risotto (recipe follows).

Plan ahead and soak this duck for the 6 hours suggested. Served warm or cold, its flavor and juiciness will astound you.

Mango Risotto

A great side dish for any simple entrée, this risotto adds a sunny flavor to the whole meal. The fresh mango pickle is made with Swedish 1-2-3 pickling solution and takes 24 hours.

For the pickle

½ cup white wine vinegar

1 cup sugar

1½ cups water

1 ripe mango, peeled, pitted, and cut into ¼-inch dice

1 shallot, minced

1 tablespoon olive oil

1 clove garlic, minced

1 cup Arborio rice

¼ cup white wine

2 cups chicken stock, simmering in a saucepan

2 scallions, green part only, sliced

1 tablespoon freshly grated Parmesan cheese

1 TO PREPARE the pickling solution, combine the vinegar, sugar, and water in a nonreactive saucepan, set over high heat, and bring the mixture to a boil, stirring until the sugar is dissolved. Remove from the heat and cool to room temperature before using. It may be refrigerated for up to 2 weeks.

2 PLACE THE diced mango into a nonreactive bowl and cover it completely with the cool pickling solution. Cover with plastic and refrigerate, covered, for 24 hours. Drain the mango and discard the brine.

3 IN A heavy, 2½-quart saucepan set over medium heat, cook the shallot in the olive oil, stirring, until translucent, about 1 minute. Add the garlic and cook, stirring, for 1 minute. Add the rice and stir well. Add the wine and stir until all the liquid is absorbed. Add one ladle of stock and continue stirring until the liquid is completely absorbed. Continue slowly adding stock and stirring until the rice is *al dente* but cooked through, about 20 minutes.

4 REMOVE FROM the heat and fold in the mango, scallions, and cheese. Taste and correct the seasonings. Ladle into warm flat soup dishes and serve at once.

Wild Strawberry Soufflés

2 to 3 tablespoons butter, melted, for
   brushing
About 2 tablespoons sugar, for dusting
1½ tablespoons water
Juice of 1 lime

1 vanilla bean, split in half lengthwise
½ cup sugar
4 large egg whites
1 cup wild strawberries, cleaned,
   stemmed, and halved

1 PREHEAT THE oven to 400°F. Brush four or five ramekins with the melted butter and sprinkle sugar inside each. Tap round to coat the bottom and sides with sugar completely. Set the ramekins on a cookie sheet.

2 BRING THE water, lime juice, vanilla bean, and sugar to a boil. Cook for 2 minutes and remove the vanilla bean.

3 BEAT THE egg whites until they form soft peaks. Strain the hot sugar syrup into the egg whites and continue beating until stiff peaks form, about 5 minutes. Fold in the strawberries.

4 GENTLY SPOON the mixture into the prepared ramekins. Bake until the soufflés are puffed and light brown on top, about 7 minutes. Serve at once, with your favorite fruit sorbet.

Intensely sweet, wild strawberries have a depth of flavor that makes all ordinary strawberries pale in comparison. Chef Samuelsson serves this soufflé with a passion fruit *granita*, but a fine fruit sorbet will do just as well.

Emiliano Sanz

Tio Pepe

Baltimore, Maryland

CONSIDER A STROLL THROUGH the sensuous gardens of the Alhambra. Contemplate sipping *sangría* on the beach of Marbella or eating fresh-caught fish at a riverside café in Seville. The enchantment of Spain can be captured on this side of the Atlantic at Tio Pepe's, where Baltimoreans, taking a break from Maryland crabs, can enjoy regional Spanish cuisine in a festive grotto in the subterranean level of two nineteenth-century buildings. The head chef, Emiliano Sanz, who is originally from Segovia in Spain, spins out specialties such as *pargo a la vasca* (red snapper in green sauce), *riñones de ternero al Jerez con arroz azafránado* (veal kidneys in sherry sauce with saffron rice), and of course classic *paella a la valenciana.*

According to Emiliano, *paella,* a typical Spanish dish filled with a variety of meats, fishes, and vegetables, blended together with rice, is also perfect to serve your señor or señorita in your own private grotto. "It is a good-looking dish that can be eaten out of the same bowl together," permitting you to linger with your date rather than hopping to and from the kitchen. *Flan al caramelo* (caramel custard) is Emiliano's choice for dessert. "In Spain, the ladies love *flan.* I don't know why," he says. "Maybe it's the texture." In any country, this sweet and creamy dish is bound to please. So mix a pitcher of Tio Pepe's *sangría* and break out the Gypsy Kings CD. It's fiesta time!

Menu

Sangría

Paella a la valenciana

Flan al caramelo

—

Sangría

⅓ cup sliced apple

⅓ cup sliced orange

⅓ cup sliced lemon

2 tablespoons sugar

3 ounces Triple Sec liqueur

3 ounces brandy

1 large bottle full-bodied red table wine

Ice cubes

Club soda

1 PLACE THE sliced fruit, sugar, Triple Sec, and brandy into a 1½- to 2-quart pitcher. Stir well until the sugar is dissolved. Stir in the wine and let the mixture stand at room temperature for 30 minutes or up to 6 hours.

2 FILL THE pitcher with ice cubes, work the spoon up and down hard enough to crush the fruit, and mix thoroughly. Taste and correct the sweetness. Add a dash of club soda to give it sparkle. Begin with *sangría* and continue drinking it throughout the dinner.

Effervescent and festive, this nectar is a blend of brandy, red wine, and Triple Sec liqueur embellished with sliced apple, orange, and lemon. Begin with *sangría* and continue drinking it throughout the evening!

Paella a la valenciana

A medley of chicken, veal, lobster, shrimp, clams, and mussels with vegetables and rice— enough to serve four or a scrumptious feast for two with plenty of leftovers for the following week. (Chef Sanz thinks it might even taste better the next day.) Prepare each of the components separately. Once combined, they bake into a compelling whole, the integrity of each flavor preserved and variety provided in each bite.

¼ cup olive oil

Half a frying chicken, cut into 4 pieces, washed, and patted dry

¼ pound veal, cut into cubes

Half a medium onion, chopped

Half a large red bell pepper, chopped

1 large clove garlic, minced

6 ounces squid, cleaned and sliced

1 cup long-grain rice

Pinch saffron, toasted for a minute in a dry skillet until fragrant

½ teaspoon salt

½ teaspoon freshly ground black pepper

2½ cups chicken stock, simmering

One 1½- to 2-pound lobster, cut into pieces

6 mussels, cleaned

4 small steamer clams, cleaned

10 raw medium shrimp, cleaned

¼ cup string beans, blanched

¼ cup green peas, defrosted

2 canned red pimientos, sliced into 1-inch-thick pieces

1 lemon, cut into wedges

1 PREHEAT THE oven to 450°F.

2 SET A *paella* pan or large ovenproof skillet over high heat, add the olive oil, and, when the oil is hot, add the chicken and the veal. Brown the meat on all sides, turning often, 5 to 8 minutes. Add the onion, bell pepper, garlic, and squid. Cook, stirring the ingredients, until they are all slightly brown, about 5 minutes. Stir in the rice, saffron, salt, and pepper, making sure the rice is coated with the oil. Pour in the stock and bring to a boil.

3 ADD THE lobster, mussels, clams, and shrimp. Bring the mixture back to the boil, add the beans and peas, and arrange the pimientos on top. Transfer the pan to the oven and bake until the seafood is cooked, about 25 minutes. Bring the *paella* to the table in its pan and serve with lemon wedges.

Flan al caramelo

For the caramel

½ cup sugar

2 cups milk	Pinch salt
½ stick cinnamon	½ cup sugar
Zest of a quarter of a lemon	Fresh raspberries (optional)
4 large eggs	

1 RINSE FIVE 4-ounce ramekins (or a 1-quart mold) in hot water and dry.

2 TO LINE the molds with caramel, melt ½ cup sugar in a small dry saucepan set over high heat. When the sugar begins to bubble, watch it closely to prevent its burning. Continue to cook until it is caramelized, about 5 minutes. Remove the pan from the heat immediately and pour the caramel into the ramekins, tilting to coat the bottom completely. Work quickly.

3 PREHEAT THE oven to 325°F. Set up a water bath: Take a pan large enough to hold all of the ramekins, half fill it with water, and set it in the oven.

4 IN A medium-heavy saucepan set over medium heat, bring the milk, cinnamon stick, and lemon zest slowly to a boil; this should take about 5 minutes. While the milk is heating, beat the eggs with the salt until they are frothy, gradually add the sugar, and continue beating until the mixture is thick and lemon colored.

5 WHEN THE milk is scalded (just at the boiling point), remove the cinnamon stick and slowly pour the hot milk into the egg mixture, beating continuously. Return the custard to the saucepan and cook over low heat, stirring constantly, until the mixture begins to thicken. Do not boil. Remove the custard from the heat, pass it through a fine-mesh sieve, and then pour it into the prepared ramekins or mold.

For this creamy flan, milk is used instead of cream and whole eggs instead of all egg yolks. A departure from the traditional vanilla, the unusual flavor comes from the lemon rind and cinnamon stick steeped in the milk.

6 PLACE THE filled molds in the water bath, adding more hot water if necessary to come halfway up the sides of the ramekins. Bake until set, when a knife inserted near the center comes out clean, about 30 minutes. To avoid holes in the flan, do not allow the water to boil. Remove the custards from the water bath and allow them to cool at room temperature. Cover and refrigerate.

7 UNMOLD THE ramekins onto pretty dessert plates. Let the ramekins rest for a few minutes on top of the flans to give the caramel time to coat and pool around the custards. Then remove the ramekins. Serve as they are or garnished with fresh raspberries.

A BOOK ABOUT FOOD and romance wouldn't be complete without a bit of advice from yours truly, Janeen Sarlin, who has helped dozens of lovesick students cook their way to romantic bliss. Cooking may be my job, but it is also my passion. I love food, the ins and outs of culinary lore, and all the flavors that come with being a chef. From my point of view, preparing an intimate dinner is the finest way to say "I love you." It's also a great way to coax him to say "I love you, too." To spin my web and ensnare my lover, I create a seductive menu of the highest quality ingredients with exciting flavors and sensuous textures. I stick to uncomplicated recipes, but I can't resist dramatic presentations.

My time to shine comes when I invite him into the kitchen to watch me cook the entrée. At my kitchen counter, he's a sitting duck—as of yet no man has not fallen for this sleight of hand. First, I pan sear the two *tournedos* of beef (men love beef, it's true). With a little flair, I transfer the steaks to a hot platter, add Madeira to the skillet, and ignite it with a wickedly long match. As I deftly tilt the pan back and forth, the flames burn out, and I look up to see the inevitable beads of sweat on his brow. Batting my eyelashes, I finish the sauce by adding exotic morels and a touch of creamy sweet butter. I spoon a bit of this lovely sauce over each *tournedo*.

As he stares in amazement, I know that I have him under my spell. Slipping off my chef jacket, I waltz out of the kitchen and into the dining room to light the candles. He pours the wine. Then I let the chips fall where they may.

Janeen A. Sarlin

Chez Sarlin
(by invitation only)

New York

Menu

Champagne—Moët & Chandon, Dom Pérignon

Smoked Salmon Pillows

Tournedos of Beef with Shallot and Morel Madeira Sauce

French Bordeaux—Château Lafite-Rothschild, 1982

Fruit with Honey and Mint Whipped Cream

Cigars and Espresso

—

Smoked Salmon Pillows

¼ pound fresh salmon fillet, skinned
  and trimmed
1 to 2 teaspoons fresh lemon juice
1 tablespoon snipped fresh chives
1 to 2 teaspoons extra virgin olive oil
Salt and freshly ground black pepper
1 tablespoon heavy cream, whipped
  with a pinch of salt until thick
  (page 14)

1 teaspoon tiny capers, drained
6 thin slices fine-quality smoked
  salmon, each approximately
  5 inches long by 1½ inches wide
4 long chive stems with blossoms
Toast points (page 11)

1 USING TWO sharp chopping knives and working on a very clean chopping board, mince the fresh salmon.

2 TRANSFER THE salmon to a small mixing bowl, stir in 1 teaspoon of the lemon juice, the snipped chives, 1 teaspoon of the olive oil, and salt and pepper. Taste and add more lemon juice and oil as needed. Gently fold the thickened cream into the salmon mixture. Stir in the capers, taste again, and correct the seasonings.

3 IF NECESSARY, press two slices of smoked salmon together to make a 1½- by 5-inch rectangle.

4 PLACE ABOUT 1 tablespoon of the "mousse" in the center of the smoked salmon. Fold the ends over to envelop the mousse and create a pillow measuring about 1½ by 1½ inches.

5 PLACE THE pillow, seam side down, on a serving plate. Count three tiny pillows per serving. Dip a pastry brush in olive oil and lightly paint the top of each pillow. Cover with plastic wrap and refrigerate until serving time.

6 TO SERVE, arrange 2 chive stems with their blossoms in a crisscross fashion over the tops of the pillows and accompany with toast points arranged in a silver basket lined with a white linen napkin.

Tournedos of Beef with Shallot and Morel Madeira Sauce

½ teaspoon dried tarragon

¼ to ½ teaspoon coarsely ground
   black pepper

2 *tournedos* of beef (6 to 8 ounces
   each), sliced about 1 inch thick
   and well trimmed

2 teaspoons Madeira

Pinch coarse sea salt

For the sauce

¼ cup Madeira

2 medium shallots, minced

8 fresh morels, washed and patted dry

¼ teaspoon chopped fresh tarragon

1 teaspoon unsalted butter, soft

> The steaks are quickly seared and set aside to rest while the sauce is made in the same pan. Flaming the Madeira evaporates most of the alcohol and enhances the rich sauce for a fast finish.

1 RUB THE tarragon and pepper into the *tournedos,* place them on a plate, and drizzle with the Madeira. Cover and let stand at room temperature for up to 1 hour or refrigerate for up to 6 hours. Remove 1 hour before cooking.

2 HEAT A nonreactive sauté pan over high heat until it is nearly smoking. Sprinkle salt on the hot pan. Add the meat and sear until it is brown on both sides, 3 to 4 minutes per side for rare, or longer according to personal preference. Transfer to a warm plate.

3 TO MAKE the sauce, add the ¼ cup Madeira to the pan. Using a long wooden match and holding your head away from the pan, carefully ignite the wine. Turn off the heat and tilt the pan back and forth carefully until the flames subside. Add the shallots and cook over medium heat until they begin to soften, about 3 minutes. Add the morels and cook, stirring, for 3 to 4 minutes longer. Add the tarragon. Remove the pan from the heat. Swirl the soft butter into the sauce to finish.

4 PLACE A *tournedo* on one side of a warm dinner plate, spoon the sauce over the meat, and serve with a medley of baby garden vegetables.

Fruit with Honey and Mint Whipped Cream

For the cream

4 fresh mint leaves, crushed

½ cup heavy cream, chilled

1 tablespoon honey

1 pint perfect wild strawberries or raspberries, wiped clean

½ pint fresh blackberries, washed

3 or 4 fresh purple figs, wiped clean and quartered

1 ripe red-skinned mango, peeled and sliced

1 FOUR OR five hours ahead, crush the mint leaves in a small bowl. Add the cream, stir well, cover with plastic wrap, and refrigerate for up to 6 hours.

2 STRAIN OUT the mint leaves through a fine-mesh strainer and stir the honey into the cream. Whip the cream until stiff.

3 SPOON THE cream into a wide, pretty glass serving bowl. Cover with plastic wrap and refrigerate until serving time.

4 ARRANGE THE fruits and berries on a pretty platter, cover with plastic wrap, and refrigerate until serving time.

5 SET OUT the platter of fruit and the bowl of cream and dip with abandon!

"WE DID A lot of champagne and oysters . . . and lots of chocolate," sighs Jimmy Schmidt remembering his courtship of Darlene, his wife of fifteen years. "We had a wild romance through food and wine. I lived in this big old house without any furniture, so we spent a lot of time cooking things like pheasant ravioli and sitting in front of the fire eating and drinking." As owner of The Rattlesnake Club, Schmidt spreads his joy of cooking for loving couples all across Detroit with his modern Midwest delicacies.

Jimmy Schmidt

The Rattlesnake Club

Detroit, Michigan

The whole purpose of a romantic meal is to create a wonderful memory. To do that, according to Schmidt, you have to activate as many senses as possible. His foolproof plan begins with the menu. Jimmy laughs when he recalls one dinner he cooked. "I didn't kill the lobsters before she came over. So she wouldn't eat, after she saw me kill them. Do yourself a favor, kill the lobsters before your date arrives. Also, if you can possibly avoid picking the lobsters up like they are hand puppets, your evening will go a lot smoother."

What's most important to Jimmy is the flow of service throughout the evening. As in a restaurant, "if a waiter is hovering over a table, it is considered bad service, equally if he's never around." Don't time out the meal. "I used to be so hyper," Schmidt says, "that I would throw the main course in the oven before we started our appetizers and, all though the first course, be thinking, 'Okay, I've got 6.5 minutes to finish before I have to take it out.'" He calls this eating to the beat and it isn't the answer. "Don't predetermine the flow. Remember it's a journey, not the destination. You are eating for the enrichment of your soul."

Menu

Oysters Poached in Champagne

Champagne—Veuve Clicquot-Ponsardin

Grilled Lobsters

Chalone California Chardonnay

Double Chocolate and Raspberry Valentines

Grand Marnier Liqueur in Champagne

Oysters Poached in Champagne

4 tablespoons unsalted butter
¼ cup sliced shallots
½ cup brut champagne or dry white wine
¼ cup bottled clam juice
⅓ cup heavy cream

10 oysters, shucked (page 9); save the lower half of the shells
Fresh seaweed, for the serving plates (available from the fish market)
Sea salt and ground white pepper
¼ cup snipped fresh chives

1 PREHEAT THE oven to 300°F. In a medium nonreactive saucepan set over high heat, melt 2 tablespoons of the butter. Add the shallots and cook, stirring, until tender, about 3 minutes. Add ¼ cup of the champagne and the clam juice and cook until reduced by half, about 12 minutes. Add the cream and cook until thickened enough to coat the back of a spoon, about 10 minutes longer. Strain through a fine-mesh strainer into a clean saucepan.

2 PLACE THE empty oyster bottom shells on a cookie sheet and set in the oven. Cover the serving plates with seaweed.

3 RETURN THE creamy sauce to medium heat and gently bring to a simmer. Add the shucked oysters and poach just until the edges begin to curl, about 2 minutes.

4 PLACE THE warmed oyster shells on the seaweed-lined serving plates, 5 shells per plate. Transfer the poached oysters to the shells and lightly tent the plates with foil to keep warm.

5 WORKING QUICKLY, whisk the remaining 2 tablespoons of butter into the simmering sauce. Add ¼ cup champagne and cook until the sauce is thick enough to coat the back of a spoon, about 3 minutes. Add salt and pepper to taste. Off the heat, stir in the chives, spoon sauce over each oyster, and serve at once.

Double Chocolate
and Raspberry Valentines

2 small oval balloons

Nonstick cooking spray

24 ounces bittersweet chocolate, for
coating and ganache

For the ganache

1¼ teaspoons unsalted butter

1½ to 1¾ cups heavy cream

1 pint fresh raspberries (half for the
filling and half for the sauce),
washed and patted dry with a
towel

¼ cup Chambord liqueur or reduced
berry juice

Powdered sugar, for garnish

2 or 3 sprigs mint, for garnish

> You needn't be an architect to execute this recipe, but it might help to practice making the molds before the big evening. Note that, after the molds are made and filled, they should be chilled for at least 8 hours before being served.

1 CLEAR THE large, open top shelf in your refrigerator. Blow up the balloons (not too large) and tie them. They should be the size of an orange. Spray the balloons very lightly with cooking spray.

2 MELT ALL of the chocolate in a metal bowl set over a pan of simmering water. Allow the chocolate to cool to 100°F. Place 2 teaspoonfuls of chocolate on a sheet pan, far enough apart to provide a perch for each chocolate-covered balloon. Dip a balloon into the warm chocolate, turning to coat the balloon evenly but leaving a little space near the tied end uncoated. Allow the excess chocolate to run off and set the balloon on one of the blobs of chocolate on the sheet pan (so the balloon will stand). Dip the second balloon and transfer the tray to the refrigerator for 15 minutes for the chocolate to harden.

3 REMOVE THE chocolate-covered balloons from the refrigerator. Puncture each of the balloons and carefully pull them out of the chocolate

189

shells. Set the shells in empty egg cartons and return them to the refrigerator while preparing the filling.

4 SET THE bowl with the remaining chocolate over a pan of simmering water. Add the butter and heat, whisking until melted. Whisk the cream into the chocolate mixture until smooth; the mixture will be quite thin. Spoon a little of this ganache into the center of each chocolate shell. Sprinkle a few raspberries over the filling. Continue layering the ganache and raspberries alternately until the shells are full. Return the shells to the refrigerator until they are set—at least 8 hours before serving.

5 PUREE THE remaining raspberries and a splash of Chambord in a food processor; sweeten with sugar to taste. Strain out the seeds, transfer the puree to an airtight container, cover, and refrigerate.

6 TO SERVE, set a chocolate shell in the center of each serving plate. Drizzle raspberry puree around the shell and onto the plate to decorate. Dust the entire plate with a little powdered sugar and garnish with a sprig of mint.

It's not unusual for the locals to spot Cory Schreiber at the farmer's market early in the morning before he goes to his restaurant, Wildwood, in Portland. The chef loves using local produce for his Northwest regional dishes. "When I'm at the farmer's market, I get a strong feeling about where the food really comes from . . . the beauty of nature."

Schreiber celebrates this passion in his own backyard garden where he grows a bounty of fruits and vegetables including several kinds of cucumbers, squashes, lettuces, tomatoes, and French beans. "My wife, Pamela, says, 'It would be nice if you spent as much time with me as you do in the garden,' " laughs Cory.

To keep himself out of the doghouse—or the greenhouse—Cory maintains domestic bliss by helping to raise their children and by cooking healthy meals for his family using treats from his garden. For quick dishes, he will toss high-quality olive oil, vinegar, and fresh herbs—"three ingredients no chef should be without"—together with pasta or potatoes. For a romantic occasion, Cory thinks mussels, a spinach salad, and a decadent white chocolate cake would do the trick.

Finding time for romance isn't always easy for the busy couple—even their son's birthday is on St. Valentine's Day, but Cory doesn't mind. "I have trunkloads of memories of time spent with my kids that I wouldn't trade for anything."

Cory Schreiber

Wildwood

Portland, Oregon

Menu

Steamed Mussels with Apples and Cider Cream
Oregon Pinot Gris—Adelsheim, Willamette Valley, 1996
Wilted Spinach Salad with Bacon, Figs, and Goat Cheese
Oregon Pinot Noir—Eyrie Vineyards, Willamette Valley, 1995
White Chocolate Cake with Warm Strawberry Sauté
Framboise—Clear Creek Distillery

191

Steamed Mussels with Apples and Cider Cream

A terrific twist on the traditional mussel appetizer, this is perfect to serve in front the fireplace on a brisk evening. Before you cook the mussels, brush thick slices of crusty bread with a bit of olive oil and grill them until they are lightly toasted. Serve the bread in a napkin-lined basket and use the slices for sopping up this marvelous sauce.

¼ cup fresh apple cider
2 shallots, finely minced
1 apple, peeled, cored, and sliced
1 pound Prince Edward Island mussels
   (or your favorite mussels),
   scrubbed

1 cup heavy cream
1 teaspoon chopped sage
1 teaspoon chopped thyme
Juice of 1 lemon
Sea salt and freshly cracked black
   pepper

1 IN A large, deep, sauté pan set over high heat, boil the apple cider until the liquid is reduced by half, about 1 minute. Add the shallots, apple, and mussels and cover the pan. Steam until the mussels open, 2 to 3 minutes. With a slotted spoon, transfer the mussels to two warm serving bowls. Lightly tent the bowls with foil and keep warm.

2 WORKING QUICKLY, add the cream to the juices remaining in the sauté pan and cook over high heat until the liquid is reduced by half, about 5 minutes. Stir in the sage, thyme, and lemon juice. Add salt and pepper to taste. Ladle the cider cream over the mussels and serve at once.

Wilted Spinach Salad
with Bacon, Figs, and Goat Cheese

4 perfect fresh figs, any variety, washed
   and stems removed

½ pound spinach, washed, stems
   removed, and spun dry

2 slices (3 to 4 ounces) smoked bacon,
   cut into 1-inch strips

1 shallot, thinly sliced

1 teaspoon Dijon mustard

¼ cup olive oil

1 tablespoon balsamic vinegar

Salt and freshly ground black pepper

2 ounces soft goat cheese

1 CUT EACH fig crosswise into 4 round slices and place in a large bowl
with the spinach.

2 COOK THE bacon in a heavy, nonreactive sauté pan set over medium
heat, stirring frequently, until it colors and turns crisp, about 5 minutes.
Add the shallot and cook for 1 minute. Stir in the mustard, olive oil, and
vinegar. Pour the hot dressing over the spinach and figs. Season with salt
and pepper and toss the salad.

3 DIVIDE THE salad between two large serving plates. Crumble the
goat cheese on top and serve.

The dazzling combination of crisp bacon, creamy goat cheese, and luscious figs atop tender spinach leaves makes this entrée salad a sure thing. Cory adds a roast squab for a heartier dish.

White Chocolate Cake
with Warm Strawberry Sauté

For the cake

¼ cup (½ stick) unsalted butter

7 ounces white chocolate

4 large eggs, separated

Pinch salt

4 tablespoons sugar

½ teaspoon pure vanilla extract

3 tablespoons Grand Marnier liqueur, plus extra for brushing

1 cup plus 2 tablespoons flour

¼ to ⅓ cup Simple Syrup (page 19)

White chocolate shavings, for garnish (page 11)

For the warm strawberry sauté

½ cup Grand Marnier liqueur

2 tablespoons sugar

1 cup sliced firm, ripe strawberries

1 tablespoon unsalted butter, softened

1 PREHEAT THE oven to 350°F. Grease a 9-inch cake pan and line the bottom with a round of parchment paper.

2 MELT THE butter and chocolate together, stirring occasionally. Set aside to cool slightly.

3 BEAT THE egg whites with the salt until frothy. Gradually add 2½ tablespoons of the sugar, beating until soft peaks form. In another bowl, beat the egg yolks until frothy, add the remaining 1½ tablespoons sugar, and beat until thick and lemon colored, about 3 minutes. Add the vanilla and liqueur. Stirring constantly, add the chocolate mixture to the yolks and mix well.

4 USING A wire whisk, fold the egg whites into the chocolate mixture one-third at a time. Fold in the flour carefully so as not to deflate the batter.

5 POUR THE cake batter into the pan and lightly tap the pan on the counter to settle the batter. Bake for 30 to 35 minutes, or until a toothpick inserted into the center comes out clean. Remove from the oven and set the cake, still in the pan, on a rack. Immediately, with a skewer, pierce the top randomly to make tiny holes. While it is still warm, brush the cake with simple syrup or additional liqueur several times. Allow the cake to cool in the pan. Before serving, remove the cake, peel off the paper, and cut into serving-size pieces. (Leftover cake wrapped in plastic can be stored, refrigerated, for 2 to 3 days.)

6 FOR THE strawberry sauté, whisk the liqueur and sugar together and pour it over the strawberries. Let the berries macerate for 15 minutes.

7 WARM THE strawberry mixture slowly over low heat. Swirl in the butter to thicken it slightly. Place a slice of cake in the center of a dessert plate, ladle some of the sauce over the top of the cake, and garnish with white chocolate shavings.

John Schumacher

Schumachers'

New Prague Hotel

New Prague, Minnesota

WHEN THE TEMPERATURES drop below freezing in Minnesota, lovers keep warm in the Schumachers' cozy hotel and restaurant. The innkeepers, John and Kathleen Schumacher, feed their guests Bavarian-themed foods such as *sauerbraten* in gingersnap sauce and *paprikás* before sending them off to bed in one of the rooms filled with hand-painted folk art furniture and lace-curtained windows. "Food and romance are the soul of what the Germans like to call gemütlichkeit or the feeling of well-being, comfort, and cordiality," says John Schumacher. "It is always a good idea to use food for romancing a special person." For John, timing is key. "Cook for someone special in your life any chance you can get—after the first date." On his menu for such an occasion would be mushrooms, veal medallions, and strawberries.

Named for his wife, Mushrooms Kathleen played an important role in the engagement of two employees. When Jeff, a former bartender, wanted to propose marriage to his girlfriend, Bernie, who worked as a desk clerk, he had John prepare a very special order of the appetizer. In addition to the four stuffed mushrooms, the chef placed the engagement ring in a raw mushroom cap in the center of the plate. Needless to say, Jeff's future wife became unglued and cried happily for the rest of the evening.

Menu

Mushrooms Kathleen

California Chardonnay—Cakebread Cellars, Napa Valley, 1996

Veal Medallions with Pink Peppercorn Sauce

Mosel Germany Riesling—Johann Josef Prüm, Wehlener Sonnenuhr Spätlese, 1996

Strawberries Brandi

California Muscat—Muscat de Beaulieu, Beaulieu Vineyard, Napa Valley

Mushrooms Kathleen

6 medium, firm white mushrooms
¼ cup butter, at room temperature
1 slice bacon, cooked crisp and
    crumbled (see Love Note)
1 small shallot, minced

1 large pinch chopped fresh parsley,
    plus more for garnish
1 clove garlic, minced
6 bay scallops, trimmed and
    patted dry
Toast points (page 11)

Discover pearl-like scallops tucked into each mushroom cap . . . or perhaps another sort of gem?

1 WASH AND dry the mushrooms and remove the stems. Set the mushrooms, hollow-side up, in a shallow baking dish that will hold them all securely in one layer.

2 SOFTEN THE butter and combine it with the bacon, shallots, parsley, and garlic.

3 PLACE ABOUT ½ teaspoon of the butter mixture in each mushroom cap and top it with one scallop. Cover each scallop with another rounded teaspoon of the butter mixture. The mushrooms may be filled up to 3 hours ahead; cover with plastic wrap and refrigerate.

4 PREHEAT THE oven to 350°F. Bake the mushrooms until they are tender but still hold their shape and are golden brown on top, about 20 minutes. Transfer the mushrooms to salad plates, garnish with a sprinkling of parsley, and serve at once with toast points.

Love Note: To cook bacon, place between paper towels and cook on high in the microwave for about 3 minutes.

Veal Medallions
with Pink Peppercorn Sauce

This delicate veal, scented with tarragon and served with a peppercorn sauce, tastes quite subtle. Pink peppercorns (a.k.a. *baies roses*) have a mildly sweet aroma but are not peppery and not unlike roses. They can be found in the spice section of good food stores. If you make the brown sauce beforehand—up to 4 weeks ahead—you can whip up this dish in about 10 minutes.

—

8 ounces veal or chicken

½ cup flour, seasoned with salt, pepper, and ¼ teaspoon dried tarragon

3 tablespoons clarified butter or canola oil

1 shallot, minced

1 teaspoon fresh lemon juice

½ cup Simple Brown Sauce (see page 20)

¼ cup dry white wine

1 teaspoon pink peppercorns

Pinch salt

Freshly ground black pepper

1 tablespoon chopped fresh parsley

1 SLICE THE veal, place the slices between two sheets of plastic wrap, and flatten them with a mallet to make medallions. Lightly dust the meat with the seasoned flour and pat off any excess.

2 HEAT THE butter in a large, heavy, nonreactive skillet set over high heat. Quickly cook the veal until it is light brown on both sides, about 1 minute per side. Transfer the veal to a plate and keep warm.

3 ADD THE shallot to the skillet and cook, stirring, until light brown, about 30 seconds. Stir in the lemon juice, brown sauce, wine, and peppercorns.

4 REDUCE THE heat to low and simmer the sauce, stirring gently, until it is reduced by half, about 4 minutes. Taste and correct the seasonings.

5 RETURN THE veal to the skillet and simmer until the meat is heated through, about 2 minutes. Transfer to warm dinner plates, sprinkle chopped parsley over, and serve at once with rice and green vegetables.

Strawberries Brandi

1 cup strawberries, plus 20 extra large
    strawberries, washed, stemmed,
    and patted dry
1 tablespoon honey
1 tablespoon powdered sugar

1 teaspoon Cointreau liqueur
1 cup heavy cream
¼ cup granulated sugar, plus extra
    for dusting
Fresh mint leaves

1 COMBINE THE 1 cup strawberries, honey, powdered sugar, and liqueur in a food processor. Process until blended, about 30 seconds. Whisk the cream with the sugar until stiff peaks form. Fold the puree into the whipped cream.

2 ROLL THE large strawberries in the granulated sugar. Arrange 10 strawberries in each serving bowl and cover with the whipped cream mixture.

What could be more romantic than spoon-feeding strawberries to a loved one?

Jim and Diana Sellers

The Catering Company
by the Sellers

Oklahoma City, Oklahoma

EVERYONE HAS HIDDEN fantasies. Jim Sellers would like to whisk his wife, Diana, away to a little whitewashed love nest on the Mediterranean, take a dip in the sea, and eat dinner right on the sand. He would prepare some of her favorite dishes from their catering company. "There is a harmonious collection of color and taste in these dishes that will really get your mouth excited," Jim says of his suggested menu.

Considering that Diana "was sold" the minute she finished their first meal together—grilled reuben sandwiches that he made one rainy weekend afternoon seven years ago—such an elaborate affair would certainly please her. But for now, he settles for a more convenient retreat, the couple's boat that is docked on Lake Ten Keller. "It's very romantic," says Jim. "We'll grill vegetables and chicken on the dock, put them in a picnic basket, and drift around on the boat. The phone doesn't even work there."

Menu

Corn and Crab Bisque

California Chardonnay—Caymus Vineyards

Swordfish with Avocado and Grapefruit Salsa

California Pinot Noir—David Bruce Winery, Estate

Apple Beignets

California—Quady Winery, Elysium Black

Corn and Crab Bisque

3 tablespoons butter

½ cup fresh corn kernels, uncooked

¼ cup chopped onion

¼ cup chopped celery

¼ cup chopped red bell pepper

1 clove garlic, minced

¼ cup flour

2½ cups vegetable stock or shellfish stock, simmering

½ cup heavy cream

¼ cup trimmed and sliced scallions

¼ cup chopped fresh parsley

¼ cup (about 2 ounces) jumbo lump crabmeat

¼ cup shredded Cheddar cheese

Salt and white pepper

Tabasco Sauce

> This beguiling bisque is hearty but not overwhelming. Served in a thermos, it would be perfect for a seashore picnic.

1 IN A large heavy saucepan set over medium heat, melt the butter, add the corn, onion, celery, bell pepper, and garlic, and cook, stirring, until the onion is softened, about 3 minutes.

2 USING A wire whisk, add the flour and stir constantly until the mixture becomes a white roux; do not brown.

3 GRADUALLY ADD the hot stock, stirring constantly until all is incorporated. Bring the soup to a low boil, reduce the heat, and simmer for 30 minutes. Remove from the heat and let stand for up to 2 hours.

4 JUST BEFORE serving, add the heavy cream, scallions, and parsley. Heat until the soup barely reaches a simmer, about 3 minutes.

5 GENTLY FOLD in the crabmeat, being careful not to break the lumps, sprinkle the cheese over the top, and fold it in. Season to taste with salt, pepper, and Tabasco Sauce. Ladle into soup bowls and serve at once.

Swordfish with Avocado and Grapefruit Salsa

2 tablespoons vegetable oil
2 cloves garlic, minced
1 tablespoon ground cumin
Salt to taste

For the salsa
1 tablespoon honey
Juice and zest of 1 lime
Half a large ripe but firm Hass
    avocado, peeled, halved, seeded,
    and cut into ¼-inch dice
1 large grapefruit, peeled and
    segmented (page 12)
Half a medium red onion, finely diced

½ teaspoon freshly ground black
    pepper
Two 6-ounce swordfish steaks

1 teaspoon canned *chipotle* chile in
    adobo sauce, seeds and
    membranes removed and
    discarded and chile minced
¼ cup chopped cilantro, plus sprigs
    for garnish
½ teaspoon ground cumin
Salt to taste

1 MIX TOGETHER the oil, garlic, cumin, salt, and pepper. Rub the mixture on the swordfish steaks, set them on a plate, cover with plastic wrap, and marinate for 10 to 15 minutes. (Refrigerate if marinating longer, up to 2 hours.)

2 FOR THE salsa, whisk the honey with the lime zest and juice. Gently toss the diced avocado in the lime mixture, cover, and reserve.

3 COMBINE THE grapefruit segments and juice, onion, minced *chipotle,* chopped cilantro, cumin, and salt, cover, and reserve.

4 PREHEAT THE broiler or grill until the coals are white hot. Grill the fish until firm to the touch, about 3 minutes on each side. Transfer to warm dinner plates and top with about ½ cup salsa. Garnish with cilantro sprigs.

Apple Beignets

1 large egg, separated, and 1 extra egg
   white
1 cup light beer
3 tablespoons canola oil
1 cup flour

½ teaspoon salt
2 Gala apples
4 cups canola oil, for frying
Whipped Cream (see page 14)

For the cardamom sugar
¼ cup sugar

½ teaspoon ground cardamom

1 WHISK TOGETHER the egg yolk, beer, and oil. In a separate bowl, whisk the egg whites until stiff peaks form. Stir the flour and salt into the egg yolk mixture, then fold in the whites. Cover and refrigerate for 1 hour.

2 FOR THE cardamom sugar, in a small bowl, combine the sugar and cardamom. Mix well and reserve.

3 JUST BEFORE serving, heat the oil in a large skillet until the temperature registers 375°F. Peel and core the apples. Cut each apple crosswise into six slices. Dip the apple into the batter. Fry one slice first to check the timing and to adjust the temperature. Lower the batter-dipped apple slices into the oil carefully and fry until golden brown, 2 to 3 minutes on each side. With a basket or slotted spoon, transfer the beignets to a baking sheet lined with paper towels to absorb excess oil.

4 ROLL OR sprinkle with cardamom sugar and serve at once. Pass the whipped cream.

Start your own Mardi Gras by serving this simple version of a New Orleans tradition. Save the batter for the morning after and serve these fritters with a cup of strong coffee.

Jeremy Sewall

The Lark Creek Inn

Larkspur, California

THE HOLIDAY SEASON at any restaurant is a busy time. For Jeremy Sewall, the executive sous-chef at The Lark Creek Inn, Christmas Eve in 1997 was particularly nerve-racking. Not only was it his girlfriend Lisa's birthday but it was also the day that he decided to ask her to marry him.

He invited Lisa and her sister, who was visiting for the holidays, to a late-night supper. "Lisa and I had hardly seen each other since early November. Restaurant plans had us all hopping," the chef remembers. After spending the day prepping and pacing in the kitchen with the velvet box tucked into the pocket of his apron, he could hardly contain himself. "All the ladies at the restaurant saw the ring before my future wife did," he confesses. "There were many oohs and ahs."

Jeremy prepared an arugula salad, scallops with curried leeks, and a free-form apple tart—Lisa's own recipe. "I chose ingredients that I knew she would love," he said. "I didn't want to propose to her and have her say, 'You know, I didn't really like the entrée.' " Sewall surprised Lisa in midcourse when he went down on one knee and asked her to marry him. When she said yes, the room exploded with cheers and clapping. "We poured magnums of champagne for every single person in the restaurant that night."

Now that they have settled down, Jeremy still likes to treat Lisa to her favorite dishes, such as homemade pasta with white truffle oil and peas. "I love to cook for her," he says. "She is so easy to please. If making pasta is the hardest thing that I have to do for her, then our marriage will be all right."

Menu

Wilted Arugula Salad with Chanterelles, Brie, and Rosemary Croutons

California Sparkling Wine—Jordan, Sparkling Wine Company, J, 1995

"Diver" Scallops with Curried Leeks and Blood Orange Sauce

California Pinot Blanc—Chalone Vineyard, 1996

Free-Form Apple Tarts with Vanilla Whipped Cream

Wilted Arugula Salad with Chanterelles, Brie, and Rosemary Croutons

2 sprigs fresh rosemary, chopped

½ cup plus 5 tablespoons extra virgin olive oil

6 round slices French bread, ½ inch thick

1 cup (about 4 ounces) chanterelles, cleaned and quartered

2 tablespoons chopped shallots

1 tablespoon minced red bell pepper

1 scallion, trimmed and thinly sliced

½ teaspoon chopped garlic

2 tablespoons minced flat-leaf (Italian) parsley

3 tablespoons balsamic vinegar

Kosher salt

Freshly ground black pepper

2 large handfuls arugula, washed

2 ounces Brie cheese, divided into 1-ounce portions, at room temperature

> The flavors of this Italian-inspired salad melt together in an operatic aria of taste and texture.
>
> —

1 COMBINE THE fresh rosemary with the ½ cup olive oil. Cover and steep for 1 hour.

2 PREHEAT THE oven to 350°F. Brush both sides of the sliced bread with the rosemary oil. Place the bread directly on the rack in the oven and bake until golden brown and crisp, 7 to 10 minutes. When cool, cut into cubes and set aside.

3 FOR THE vinaigrette, heat 4 tablespoons olive oil in a nonreactive sauté pan set over high heat. Add the chanterelles and cook, shaking the pan, until golden brown, about 4 minutes. Remove the chanterelles and set aside. To the same pan over medium heat, add the shallots, bell pepper, scallion, and garlic and cook, stirring constantly, for 1 minute. If the vegetables begin to color, reduce the heat. Return the chanterelles to the pan and remove from the heat.

continued

4 STIR THE parsley and balsamic vinegar into the hot vegetables. Slowly add the remaining tablespoon of olive oil, stirring constantly. Season with salt and pepper.

5 DIVIDE THE arugula between 2 shallow serving bowls. Lean the Brie against the greens. Spoon warm vinaigrette over both salads, top with the croutons, and serve at once.

"Diver" Scallops with Curried Leeks and Blood Orange Sauce

2½ cups blood orange juice or regular orange juice

3 sprigs fresh thyme

4 tablespoons unsalted butter, softened

2 large leeks, white part only, washed and julienned

3 tablespoons curry powder

3 tablespoons olive oil

10 ounces fresh sea scallops, washed and patted dry with paper towels (page 13)

Kosher salt

Freshly ground black pepper

1 IN A nonreactive saucepan set over high heat, bring the orange juice and thyme to a boil. Cook until reduced to ½ cup liquid, 8 to 10 minutes. Strain, return the sauce to the pan, and set aside.

2 IN A sauté pan set over low heat, melt 2 tablespoons of the butter. Add the leeks and cook slowly, stirring frequently, for 3 minutes. Add the curry powder and continue cooking until the leeks are tender, about 5 minutes.

3 HEAT THE olive oil in a cast-iron or other heavy skillet over high heat. Season the scallops with salt and pepper. When the oil is lightly smoking, sear the scallops until golden brown on both sides, about 3 minutes total.

4 REHEAT THE reduced juice until it boils, remove from the heat, and rapidly whisk in the remaining 2 tablespoons of butter.

5 MOUND THE leeks in the center of two warm plates. Arrange the scallops on top of the leeks and circle the scallops with the sauce. Serve at once.

The mild sweetness of curry-seasoned leeks works magic with the succulence of fresh sea scallops. Larger than bay scallops, sea scallops make a delectably light entrée, especially when complemented by a ruby orange sauce.

Free-Form Apple Tarts with Vanilla Whipped Cream

For the crust

2½ cups all-purpose flour

1 teaspoon salt

¾ cup (1½ sticks) unsalted butter, chilled and cut into pieces

¼ cup vegetable shortening, chilled

6 tablespoons ice water

For the filling

½ tablespoon ground cinnamon

2 tablespoons sugar

⅛ teaspoon ground cloves

⅛ teaspoon grated nutmeg

3 tart baking apples, such as Granny Smith

2 tablespoons fresh lemon juice

Whipped Cream (see page 14), for garnish

1 MIX THE flour and salt in a food processor. Add the cold butter and shortening and cut them into the flour until it resembles coarse meal. Do not overprocess. Transfer the mixture to a bowl, make a well in the center, add the ice water, and mix with a fork until the mixture comes together in a ball. Wrap the ball in plastic and chill for at least 1 hour.

2 PREHEAT THE oven to 400°F.

3 FOR THE filling, mix together the cinnamon, sugar, cloves, and nutmeg. Peel and core the apples, cut them into thin slices, and toss the slices in the lemon juice and then in the sugar mixture.

4 CUT THE dough in half and roll out into two ⅛- to ¼-inch-thick circles about 12 inches across. Place the circles on a greased baking sheet. Spoon half of the filling in the center of each dough circle. Fold the edges of the dough over the apples, leaving a 1- to 1½-inch circular-opening at the center. (This is free form.) Bake until the apples are tender and the crust is golden brown, about 20 minutes. Remove from the oven and let cool for 4 to 5 minutes. Serve hot, warm, or at room temperature.

5 TO SERVE, slide the tarts onto pretty dessert plates and top with vanilla-flavored whipped cream.

Allen Susser

Chef Allen's

Aventura, Florida

PERHAPS IT IS because so many New Yorkers, accustomed to fine dining, eventually migrate to Miami, or perhaps it is because the locals got really tired of frozen fish and Key lime pie, but, in the past decade, New World restaurants, blending Caribbean with traditional American ingredients, have popped up in the sunshine state like whitecaps in the sea. Some, sadly, have sunk to the bottom of the ocean; others have made quite a big splash. One of the restaurants riding the crest is Chef Allen's.

Innovative versions of tropical fish flavored with mango, papaya, tangerine, and coconut have given Allen Susser his status as a celebrity chef. Not bad for a guy who began his career flipping burgers and dogs at an amusement park in Queens, New York. Considered one of the more romantic spots to dine, Chef Allen's is actually tucked away in a strip mall. The art deco dining room is shaded pink with neon trim—this is Miami—and is well air-conditioned. But the candles and the white tablecloths signify seduction.

At home, Chef Susser would suggest a similar setting. "Put down a linen tablecloth and a nice candle. Don't forget to bring out your best china and glassware," he prescribes. For dinner, he would serve his wife, Judi, who is "an inspiration to his cooking," tuna poke, lobster strudel, and red banana brûlée—a cornucopia of fusion foods. "The meal is exotic and the color and textures give you something to talk about."

Susser's cooking style resembles his philosophy about romance. "It's about balance," he says. "Judi and I love traveling together. We try to get away once a year on vacation to places like Napa, Hawaii, or Paris." On a daily basis, amidst the hustle of running the business and raising kids, "we try to find a few minutes for each other just sitting at home."

Menu

Tuna Poke with Key Lime and Coconut

Lobster Strudel with Chayote and Almonds

California Chardonnay—Newton Vineyard, 1997

Red Banana Brûlée with Clementine Fruit Salsa

California Late-Harvest Sémillon—Far Niente, Dolce, 1994

Tuna Poke with Key Lime and Coconut

1 tablespoon minced fresh ginger

½ teaspoon minced garlic

1 tablespoon sesame oil

½ tablespoon minced hot Thai chile
   or jalapeño pepper

1 tablespoon minced scallion

1 tablespoon minced cilantro, plus
   sprigs for garnish

1 tablespoon soy sauce

½ pound fresh tuna fillet, diced into
   medium-size chunks

1 tablespoon Key lime juice

2 tablespoons shaved fresh coconut,
   toasted (see Love Note)

Poke is a preparation of extremely fresh fish or seafood simply marinated and chilled.

1 COMBINE THE ginger and garlic. In a small saucepan set over high heat, warm the sesame oil until it shimmers, about 30 seconds, and add it to the garlic and ginger; mix well. Add the chile, scallion, minced cilantro, soy sauce, and tuna. Mix well. Cover the bowl and refrigerate for at least 2 hours.

2 JUST BEFORE serving, stir the lime juice and coconut into the mixture. Divide the poke between 2 serving plates and garnish with a sprig of cilantro.

Love Note: To prepare fresh coconut meat, pierce the three eyes with a nail and hammer and drain out the liquid. Place the coconut in a 350°F oven for exactly 15 minutes. Slip the coconut into a plastic bag and then into a brown paper bag and crack open the shell with a good whack of the hammer. Pry the meat from the shell and pare off the dark inner skin. Using a vegetable peeler, shave off the amount of coconut that will used. Store the remaining pieces of coconut in a Ziploc bag and freeze for up to 3 months. Toast the coconut in a heavy dry skillet over moderate heat, constantly tossing or stirring the shavings until they are brown, 3 to 4 minutes. Transfer to paper towels.

Lobster Strudel with Chayote and Almonds

For the strudel

1 large lobster tail, cooked and
    chopped (1 generous cup)
1 small shallot, minced
Quarter of stalk celery, diced
Quarter of medium red bell pepper,
    seeded and diced

1 tablespoon brandy
½ teaspoon salt
½ teaspoon freshly ground black
    pepper
3 sheets phyllo dough
2 tablespoons olive oil

For the garnish

About ½ large chayote, peeled and
    julienned
1 or 2 Anaheim chiles, julienned
About ½ medium mango, peeled and
    julienned

2 tablespoons (1 ounce) slivered
    almonds
Salt and freshly ground black pepper
Few stalks fresh chives, minced
    (1 teaspoon)

1 COMBINE THE lobster meat, shallot, celery, red pepper, brandy, salt, and pepper. Mix well and set aside.

2 TO ASSEMBLE the strudel, layer the phyllo sheets on top of one another, brushing olive oil between each layer. Cut the stack in half lengthwise. Divide the lobster stuffing between the two halves, placing the mixture at one end of each strip and spreading it out over one-third of the dough. Roll up each strudel jelly-roll style, enclosing the filling. Brush each roll with olive oil and place, seam-side down, on a greased baking sheet.

3 PREHEAT THE oven to 375°F. Bake the strudels on the center rack in the center of the oven until golden brown, about 7 minutes. Remove from the oven and let stand about 5 minutes before slicing.

4 WHILE THE strudels are baking, prepare the vegetables. Cook the chayote in the remaining olive oil in a sauté pan set over high heat, stirring, for 1 minute. Add the chiles, mango, and almonds and cook, stirring constantly, for 1 minute. Season with salt and pepper to taste. Cook about 2 minutes longer, until the vegetables are just tender. Sprinkle with chives.

5 TO SERVE, spoon the chayote mixture onto two colorful warm plates. Cut each strudel on the bias and place the slices directly on the chayote mixture.

Red Banana Brûlée
with Clementine Fruit Salsa

For the salsa

1 large clementine or tangerine, segmented (page 12)

Half a medium grapefruit, segmented (page 12)

Half a medium mango

1 tablespoon honey

1 tablespoon brewed orange pekoe tea

2 teaspoons almonds, toasted (page 12)

2 medium, ripe red bananas

1 teaspoon freshly squeezed lime juice

⅛ teaspoon pure vanilla extract

1 tablespoon light brown sugar

2 sprigs fresh mint, for garnish

1 CUT THE clementine and grapefruit segments into thirds and place in a stainless-steel bowl. Peel, seed, and cut the mango into ¼-inch dice. Add the mango to the citrus fruit, along with the honey, tea, and almonds and mix well. Cover and refrigerate until cold.

2 TO PREPARE the bananas, peel them carefully—the skin is just a bit thicker than that of an ordinary yellow banana. Split the bananas in half lengthwise and place them in a flat glass ovenproof dish, cut side up. Whisk together the lime juice and vanilla. Using a pastry brush, coat the bananas with the lime mixture. Generously spoon the brown sugar over the bananas.

3 PREHEAT THE broiler. When it is very hot, broil the bananas for 2 to 3 minutes, until the sugar is caramelized. Watch carefully; it will burn easily. Let the bananas cool for 1 minute before removing them from the dish.

4 DIVIDE THE fruit salsa between 2 serving bowls. Place 2 halves of the banana brûlée on top of the salsa and garnish with a sprig of fresh mint.

The red-skinned red banana has a more aromatic vanilla flavor than its yellow cousin. The addition of lime and brown sugar, burnt together, add a new dimension of flavor.

If you want to make a good impression on a first date, find a yummy out-of-the-way bistro that's warm and intimate, so that when you run out of things to talk about, you can eavesdrop on the diners next to you. Audrey Claire, a tiny treasure in the heart of the city of brotherly love that, incidentally, won "Best First-Date Place" category from *Philadelphia* magazine in 1998, is just the place. Open the door to find an oasis painted soft meadow green and bathed in pumpkin-colored sunlight. Mediterranean perfumes of onions and olive oil spilling out of the open-air kitchen greet you and your date at the door. Nibble on pancakes of chickpeas and shrimp, chickens glazed in pomegranate molasses, and pasta tossed in tomatoes and fresh peas.

A modern-day Snow White, but with longer hair and wearing a denim shirt, will approach your table to ask how you are doing. This is the young proprietor, Audrey Claire Taichman. "I always wanted to own this kind of restaurant," she explains. "I just wish that I could be a customer sometimes."

Audrey grew up watching her mother cook and chose to read *Gourmet* magazine instead of *Glamour*. After several waitressing stints, she knew it was time to open up her dream eatery. Now that she has, she is hoping that Mr. Quite Possibly will walk through the glass door. When he does, she will treat him to a menu like the one below. The apple cake, a favorite on the menu, is her mother's recipe. "It's really moist, really comforting, and makes a good conversation piece."

If you are cooking for someone special, Audrey has a couple of suggestions: "Always act as if you know what you're doing even if you don't. Toasting your own pine nuts is really simple to do," and they're sophisticated enough to impress your date, making you look as if "you really know something about food."

Audrey Claire
Taichman

Audrey Claire

Philadelphia

Menu

Baby Arugula Salad with Fresh Figs, Raspberries, French Lentils, and Warm Goat Cheese

Pappardelle with Portobello Mushrooms, Arugula, Pine Nuts, and Shaved *Locatelli*

California Chardonnay—Sonoma-Cutrer Vineyard, Russian River Valley

Bubbie's Apple Cake

❦

215

Baby Arugula Salad with Fresh Figs, Raspberries, French Lentils, and Warm Goat Cheese

For the dressing

2 tablespoons red wine vinegar

1 tablespoon honey

¼ cup vegetable oil

1½ tablespoons olive oil

1½ tablespoons hazelnut oil

2 tablespoons crushed hazelnuts, toasted (page 12)

Salt and freshly ground black pepper

2 ounces green French lentils, cooked and drained (canned is fine; drain well)

Extra virgin olive oil, for drizzling

2 slices goat cheese, 1 ounce each

6 ounces baby arugula, washed and spun dry

10 raspberries

4 fresh figs, cut in half

1 TO MAKE the dressing, whisk the vinegar together with the honey and slowly add the oils. Stir in the hazelnuts and add salt and pepper to taste.

2 ADD A tablespoon of the dressing to the lentils and marinate for at least 10 minutes.

3 PREHEAT THE broiler. Line a baking sheet with foil, drizzle oil on the foil, set the cheese on the foil, and drizzle a few more drops of oil over the cheese. Set aside.

4 TOSS THE arugula with just enough dressing to coat the leaves. Divide the greens neatly onto two large plates. Set the pan with the cheese under the broiler until the cheese is warm but not melted, about 2 minutes.

5 PLACE THE raspberries and figs around the edges of the arugula. Place the warm cheese in the center of the greens, sprinkle the lentils over the top, and drizzle a few drops of dressing on the cheese. Serve at once.

Pappardelle with Portobello Mushrooms, Arugula, Pine Nuts, and Shaved *Locatelli*

1 large portobello mushroom
1 tablespoon butter
1 clove garlic, minced
Salt and freshly ground black pepper
4 ounces fresh *pappardelle*, uncooked
1½ tablespoons extra virgin olive oil

1 ounce fresh arugula, washed and
   spun dry, tough stems removed
2 tablespoons pine nuts, toasted
   (page 12)
¼ to ⅓ cup shaved *Locatelli* romano
   cheese

1 PREHEAT THE oven to 475°F. Roast the mushroom with the butter, garlic, and salt and pepper to taste until tender, about 15 minutes. Remove from the oven and slice thinly.

2 COOK THE fresh pasta in boiling salted water until *al dente*, about 3 minutes.

3 HEAT THE olive oil in a large skillet over high heat. Add the roasted mushroom and stir for 1 to 2 minutes. Add the arugula and more oil if necessary, and cook until wilted, about 2 minutes. Season with salt and pepper to taste. Add the drained pasta to the skillet and toss evenly with the vegetables. Add a splash of pasta water to the skillet to create a sauce. Transfer the pasta to warm pasta bowls or serving plates, sprinkle with the pine nuts and cheese shavings and serve at once.

This is the perfect whip-up-a-little-something dish. After spending the day together, pop by the market and pick up some fresh pasta and the vegetables. It's quick, simply delicious, and there is no special equipment necessary.

217

Bubbie's Apple Cake

Vegetable shortening, for greasing
5 medium firm apples (preferably Golden Delicious), peeled, cored, and sliced (6 rounded cups)
5 tablespoons plus 1 cup sugar
5 teaspoons cinnamon
3 cups all-purpose flour
3 teaspoons baking powder
1 teaspoon salt
4 large eggs, beaten
¼ cup orange juice
2 tablespoons pure vanilla extract
1 cup vegetable oil

1 PREHEAT THE oven to 375°F. Grease a 10-inch angel-food cake pan or large Bundt pan generously with vegetable shortening.

2 COMBINE THE apples with the 5 tablespoons of sugar and the cinnamon. Set aside.

3 SIFT TOGETHER the flour, the remaining 1 cup sugar, the baking powder, and salt. Whisk the eggs, add the orange juice, vanilla, and oil, and mix well. Make a well in the center of the flour mixture, pour the egg mixture into the well, and stir until well blended. The batter will be very stiff.

4 SPOON ONE-THIRD of the batter into the bottom of the prepared pan, spreading it evenly. Drain off any liquid from the apples and place half of the apples evenly on top of the batter. Repeat the process once again, ending by covering the second half of the apples with the remaining batter. Smooth the top with a rubber scraper. Bake until firm and a cake tester comes out clean, about 1 hour and 15 to 20 minutes. Remove from the oven and cool to lukewarm in the pan, about 1 hour. Turn the cake out onto a serving plate. Serve it warm, topped with whipped cream or ice cream, or simply dust the top with powdered sugar.

It WAS OVER thirty years ago that Michael Terry, a law student at Harvard, kissed his new bride, Elizabeth, to thank her for the delicious dinner she had just made, and headed back out to the law library. Elizabeth, who was still getting her kitchen legs, decided to tackle the wonderful world of baking. Her husband returned that evening to find two plump blueberry pies cooling on a windowsill. Michael led his wife to their bed, where they fed each other mouthfuls of flaky crust and steaming fresh blueberries.

Since 1980, the Terrys have called Elizabeth on 37th home. They occupy the rooms upstairs from the restaurant that is housed in a graceful turn-of-the-century mansion in Savannah's historic district. It's a real family affair. "The staff practically raised my daughters," says Elizabeth. Michael, who has since given up his successful law practice, plays host and wine expert while Elizabeth works behind the scenes, creating innovative new Southern cuisine.

A visit to this restaurant is like slipping into an old Hollywood movie. You almost expect to see Vivien Leigh in a hoop skirt strolling through the grand entrance hall on the arm of Clark Gable. Symmetrical dining rooms finished in rich colors and elegant trim are perfect backdrops.

Michael and Elizabeth have to take their work home with them, for obvious reasons, but they are careful to take time out for themselves, enjoying an occasional glass of champagne together on their beloved porch. Is that the secret ingredient in their happy marriage? Elizabeth proposes that it is about consistency. "Instead of adding spice to your routine, keep the routine spicy . . . I find that Michael and I are still growing and changing together even after thirty-four years. It's wonderfully romantic."

Menu

Broiled Mustard-Glazed Fish
with Curried Onions, Tomatoes, and Green Beans

Blueberry Pie

German Riesling gba, Wilhelm Weil, Rheingau, 1997

219

Broiled Mustard-Glazed Fish with Curried Onions, Tomatoes, and Green Beans

5 tablespoons extra virgin olive oil
1 tablespoon balsamic vinegar
1 tablespoon soy sauce
2 tablespoons Dijon mustard

1 teaspoon fresh cracked black pepper
Two 6-ounce fillets tuna or salmon, cut 1 inch thick

For the vegetables

⅓ pound fresh green beans
1 tablespoon freshly grated Parmesan cheese
1 tablespoon butter
1 teaspoon curry powder

1 Vidalia or sweet Spanish onion, peeled and julienned
1 large, perfectly firm, ripe garden tomato
Sliced French bread

1 PREPARE THE glaze by whisking together 4 tablespoons of the olive oil, the vinegar, soy sauce, mustard, and pepper. Set aside.

2 STEAM THE green beans over simmering water until they are crunch tender, 4 to 5 minutes. Plunge into cold water to stop the cooking process and drain well. Toss the beans with 1 tablespoon of the glaze. Sprinkle with the Parmesan cheese and set aside in a warm place.

3 IN A medium nonreactive skillet set over medium heat, warm the butter, the remaining tablespoon of olive oil, and the curry powder for about 2 minutes. Add the onion and cook, stirring, until crisp tender, about 5 minutes. Do not allow to brown. Set aside to cool.

4 PREHEAT THE grill or broiler to high. Spoon the rest of the glaze over both sides of the fish. Place the fish on a broiler pan, about 4 inches from the heat, and broil, turning once, cooking until only a ribbon of pink shows in the center of the fish, about 5 minutes on each side. Or grill over white-hot coals, about 5 minutes on each side.

5 CUT THE tomato into thin crosswise slices about ¼ inch thick. Arrange the tomatoes on two large dinner plates next to a mound of green beans. Spoon the curried onions on top of the tomato and place a fish fillet in the center of the plate. Serve at once with French bread.

Blueberry Pie

This is the pie that sealed eternal honeymoon bliss for Elizabeth and her husband. May it work its simple wonder for you, too.

—

For the crust

3 cups all-purpose flour

1 teaspoon salt

1 cup unsalted butter, very cold, cut
    into small pieces

1 large egg

About 3 tablespoons ice water

For the filling

2 pints fresh blueberries, picked over,
    washed, and drained
    (about 4 cups)

2 tablespoons cornstarch

3 tablespoons quick-cooking tapioca

1 cup sugar

½ teaspoon cinnamon

1 tablespoon fresh lemon juice

1 MIX THE flour and salt together in a food processor. Add the cold butter and process until the mixture resembles a coarse meal. Transfer to a mixing bowl. Whisk together the egg and about 2 tablespoons of ice water. Pull the liquid through the flour, adding more water as necessary, until the mixture forms a ball. Wrap the ball of dough in plastic and refrigerate for at least 30 minutes, or up to 4 hours.

2 PREHEAT THE oven to 375°F. Remove the dough from the refrigerator and cut it in half. Working on a floured surface, flatten one half with your hands, then roll into a circle large enough to line a 9-inch buttered pie pan, leaving about a 1-inch overhang around the edge. Cover with plastic wrap and chill.

3 TO MAKE the filling, combine 1 cup of the blueberries with the cornstarch, tapioca, sugar, cinnamon, and lemon juice. Bring to a boil and cook, stirring constantly, until the mixture is thick and shiny, about 3 minutes. Remove from the heat and set aside to cool for 10 minutes. Stir in the remaining 3 cups of blueberries. Spoon into the cold, unbaked bottom crust.

4 ROLL OUT the second crust and cut it into strips. Place the strips on top of the berry filling to form a lattice pattern. Crimp the edges decoratively.

5 PLACE THE pie in the center of the oven, with a sheet pan or cookie sheet on the shelf below to catch any dripping juices. Bake until the fruit bubbles and the crust is brown, about 50 minutes. Cool on a rack before cutting.

Norman Van Aken

Norman's

Coral Gables, Florida

WHEN NORMAN VAN AKEN was twenty years old, he plunged head-first into the culinary world as a breakfast cook at a diner in Libertyville, Illinois. There he came down with a bad case of puppy love for a timid seventeen-year-old waitress named Janet. When Janet decided to quit school and move to Florida, Norman wasn't far behind. In Key West, Norman took a job for three bucks an hour at an all-night barbecue called the Midget Bar and Grill.

On Janet's birthday, he took her to Louie's Backyard, one of the best restaurants in town. When dinner ended, it was back to the Midget for him. Janet tagged along, hoping to share a few more moments with her date. She got more than she bargained for. When the dishwasher didn't show up, Janet rolled up her sleeves and rinsed dishes until dawn. They've been side by side ever since.

At Norman's, Janet inspires her husband, helping him plan menus and test recipes. She even washes dishes. His mind wanders back to the early days when they spent their time in Key West, walking through the old streets holding hands or staring out into the ocean while sipping Cuban coffee. He takes a deep sigh and simply says, "I married the right woman."

To feed your lover, Norman has created a New World feast of caviar on cheese crisps and yellowtail with garlicky mashed potatoes. If you are unable to locate yellowtail, you can always substitute another white fish. Just make sure that it is delicate. "You want it to cuddle on the potatoes, not sit stiff on top like a surfboard."

Menu

Truffled Manchego Wafers with Beluga Caviar

Fillet of Yellowtail Snapper with Garlicky Mashed Potatoes, Asparagus, and Citrus Butter

Billecart-Salmon, Blanc de Blancs, Mareuil-sur-Ay, 1990

Chocolate Truffles

224

Truffled Manchego Wafers with Beluga Caviar

8 tablespoons unsalted butter

1½ tablespoons sugar

3 large egg whites, unbeaten

1½ tablespoons roasted garlic
   (page 12)

¾ teaspoon salt

1 cup plus 2½ tablespoons flour

¼ generous cup Manchego cheese,
   finely grated

1 tablespoon truffle oil

1 ounce beluga caviar (or the best you
   can afford)

1 PREHEAT THE oven to 375°F. Line a cookie sheet with parchment paper and set aside.

2 CREAM THE butter and sugar together in a food processor until fluffy. Add the egg whites and garlic and pulse briefly. Add the salt, flour, cheese, and truffle oil. Pulse again briefly. Transfer to a clean bowl, cover with plastic wrap, and refrigerate for 30 minutes.

3 SPOON TEASPOON-SIZE dollops of the batter onto the prepared pan, as if making cookies. Using your fingers, smear the batter round, making 2-inch circles of batter. Bake until the wafers are varying degrees of brown, 8 to 12 minutes.

4 TO SERVE, top each wafer with a spoonful of caviar.

Love Note: This batter makes about 5½ dozen 2-inch wafers. We recommend that you mix up the whole recipe, bake as many wafers as you want for the evening, and freeze the rest of the batter (pressed in circles, between parchment) for another lovely caviar moment.

Made from sheep's milk, Manchego, semifirm and mild, is Spain's most famous cheese. Its richness suits the nutty aroma of truffle oil and it melts beautifully into these wafers.

Fillet of Yellowtail Snapper with Garlicky Mashed Potatoes, Asparagus, and Citrus Butter

Golden yellowtail snapper glazed in a light citrus butter is served on a fluffy pillow of garlicky mashed potatoes and accompanied by spring-green asparagus—a sensuous meal that will arouse the taste buds and comfort the soul.

—

For the citrus butter

½ cup freshly squeezed orange juice

3 tablespoons champagne vinegar

2 shallots, sliced

1 bay leaf, broken

1 teaspoon freshly cracked black
    pepper

3 tablespoons heavy cream

½ pound (2 sticks) butter, cut into
    small pieces and kept very cold

For the potatoes

6 to 8 new potatoes, peeled and diced

1 cup heavy cream

1½ tablespoons butter

2 tablespoons roasted garlic
    (page 12)

Coarse salt and freshly ground black
    pepper

For the fish

1 large egg

¼ cup half-and-half

Coarse salt and freshly ground black
    pepper

Two 8-ounce fillets yellowtail snapper
    or other thin, delicate fish

¼ cup flour

⅛ cup clarified butter or canola oil

½ pound fresh asparagus, trimmed,
    peeled, and cooked *al dente*

1 SIMMER THE orange juice, vinegar, shallots, bay leaf, and cracked pepper together until the liquid is reduced to about 6 tablespoons, about 10

226

minutes. Add the heavy cream. Once it boils, whisk in the butter, a little bit at a time, until incorporated. Remove from the heat, strain through a fine-mesh strainer, and keep the sauce in a warm place.

2 BOIL THE potatoes until tender and drain well. In a medium sauce-pan set over high heat, bring the cream to a boil and whisk in the roasted garlic and the butter. Reduce the heat and simmer until the liquid is reduced to ½ cup, about 8 minutes. Mash the potatoes, adding the garlic cream little by little. Taste and correct the seasoning. Keep warm until ready to serve.

3 PREHEAT THE oven to 425°F. Whisk the egg with the half-and-half and add the salt and pepper. Set aside. Dust the fish fillets with flour, being sure to spank off any excess. Place the fillets into the egg wash and let sit until ready to cook. This may be done up to 2 hours ahead.

4 HEAT THE clarified butter in a large sauté pan set over medium-high heat. Lift the fish out of the egg wash and transfer to the hot butter. Cook the fish until golden brown, 1 to 2 minutes on each side. Transfer the fillets to a baking pan and bake until the flesh is opaque and firm to the touch, 5 to 8 minutes.

5 PLACE A mound of mashed potatoes in the center of two plates. Top the potatoes with a fish fillet and ladle citrus butter over the top. Arrange the asparagus around the edge of the plate and serve at once. Pass extra cit-rus butter at the table.

Johnny Vinczencz

Astor Place Bar and Grill

Miami, Florida

OCEAN DRIVE IN South Beach, Miami, offers the best spot for people watching. Park yourself at one of the outdoor cafés, order a martini, and enjoy the parade of scantily clad models strutting by. When you're ready for dinner, head up the block to Astor Place Bar and Grill, where the chef, Johnny Vinczencz, will create a sublime feast of cowboy-Caribbean cuisine.

Unlike neighboring restaurants housed in flamingo-pink buildings, Astor Place is situated in the lower level of the sleek Hotel Astor. The marble and limestone lobby with art deco accents evokes the Silver Screen era.

Johnny Vinczencz, sporting chef whites and a baseball cap, knows the advantage that chefs have when playing the field. "For me, cooking dinner for a lady has sort of been my ace in the hole," he boasts. "It's a great ice breaker, and, as a chef, I can make a four-course meal in twenty minutes." This usually happens on the third date. "It's too much for the first date, by the second date you're still not sure, but if you make it to the third date it's time to open the relationship up and see what's going to happen." To avoid any mishaps, Johnny plans dinner carefully. "Women can be finicky about what they can and cannot eat; men seem to say, 'Food? Sounds great!' I like cooking seafood—women tend to eat that more than, let's say, a steak."

One of his creations is the South Beach Picnic Basket, an assortment of treasures from the sea such as lobster tails, stone crab claws, and shrimp with mustard and *chipotle* dipping sauces. Fill the basket and head to the beach, to the park, or the backyard on a warm evening. There are no set rules. Just reach in and take what you want.

Menu

Shucked "White Water" Oysters (see page 9)

South Beach Seafood "Picnic" Basket with Lobster Tail, Stone Crab Claws, Fresh Shrimp with Mustard and Chipotle Dipping Sauces

Mango Coleslaw

Smoked Rock-Shrimp Potato Salad

Italian Pinot Grigio Villa Rusiz, Collio, 1997

Strawberries with Grand Marnier Liqueur

Seafood "Picnic" Basket with Two Dipping Sauces

Chipotle Cocktail Dipping Sauce

1 cup chile sauce

½ cup ketchup

3 canned *chipotle* chiles in adobo sauce

¼ cup shredded fresh horseradish

½ teaspoon Worcestershire sauce

Juice of 1 lime

Sea salt and freshly ground black
    pepper

MIX ALL the ingredients together in a food processor or blender, transfer to a clean jar, and refrigerate until ready to serve. Serve with cold seafood.

Mustard Dipping Sauce

1 cup mayonnaise

3½ teaspoons Colman's dry mustard

1 teaspoon Worcestershire sauce

½ cup spicy brown mustard

3 tablespoons honey

2 tablespoons sour cream

Salt and freshly ground black pepper

MIX ALL the ingredients together, transfer to a clean jar, and refrigerate until ready to serve. Serve with cold seafood.

Ask your fishmonger to cook your favorite seafood such as lobster tails, stone crab claws, and shrimp. Keep refrigerated until ready to serve the feast. Arrange the seafood in airtight containers and pack it in an insulated cooler to place inside your wicker basket.

229

Mango Coleslaw

1 firm ripe mango

½ cup mayonnaise

1 teaspoon white wine vinegar

2 teaspoons fresh lime juice

About 1 tablespoon sugar

Coarse salt and freshly ground black
  pepper

2 generous cups shredded white
  cabbage

½ cup generous cup shredded red
  cabbage

1 carrot, julienned

About 12 cilantro leaves, chopped

1 PEEL THE mango, cut a quarter of it into julienne strips, and set aside. Puree half of the remainder of the mango flesh in a food processor. Transfer the purée to a small bowl and add the mayonnaise, vinegar, lime juice, and sugar. Mix well. Add salt and pepper to taste.

2 TOSS THE white and red cabbage together with the carrots. Add the cilantro and julienned mango. Stir the mango dressing into the cabbage mixture and toss well. Add salt and pepper to taste. Cover and refrigerate until ready to serve.

Smoked Shrimp Potato Salad

Coarse salt

2 large baking potatoes, peeled and
diced

Half a medium yellow bell pepper,
diced

Half a medium red bell pepper, diced

Half a medium green bell pepper,
diced

6 fresh basil leaves, cut into slivers

1 tablespoon chopped cilantro leaves

4 scallions, trimmed and diced

2 stalks celery, diced

⅓ cup diced red onion

¾ to 1 pound smoked rock shrimp

¼ cup mayonnaise, or more if
necessary

2 tablespoons olive oil

Freshly ground black pepper

1 IN A medium saucepan set over high heat, bring 4 cups of water to a
boil. Add about 1 teaspoon of salt and boil the diced potatoes until tender,
about 15 minutes; drain.

2 COMBINE THE yellow, red, and green pepper, basil, cilantro, scallions, celery, and onions. Stir in the smoked shrimp. Dress with mayonnaise
and olive oil and season with salt and pepper. Add the potatoes and mix.
Add more mayonnaise if necessary to bind all the ingredients. Taste and
correct the seasonings. Cover with plastic wrap and refrigerate until serving
time.

Smoked shrimp and a rainbow of peppers add flavor to traditional potato salad. Smoked rock shrimp is available in gourmet stores; use regular small shrimp instead only as a last resort.

Susan Weaver

Fifty Seven Fifty Seven
Restaurant and Bar

New York

Love in the afternoon never tasted as good as Susan Weaver's Tea for Two of enchanting sweets and sandwiches. "This food isn't subtle," says Susan, who plays Queen of Hearts every St. Valentine's Day, when pairs come to Fifty Seven Fifty Seven in the Four Seasons Hotel to enjoy the late-afternoon treat.

A romantic tea at home is a charming alternative to a full-blown dinner. "It's wonderful to slip away in the afternoon and have lots of little things to eat," says Susan. Rather than serve a formal tea in your dining room, plop down on the living room floor in front of a crackling fire.

Everyone knows that you can tell how a man will treat you by the way he treats his mother. But did you know that you can tell how he will behave by his conduct in a restaurant? Check out your date next time you're dining together. How does he treat the staff? What is his choice of wine? Susan prefers suitors who don't skimp. "If I go out with a guy and he orders a jug of house wine and wants to split a salad and an entrée, then . . . there won't be any dessert."

The same adage holds true for homespun spreads. "I love when people cook their mothers' recipes. You can tell a lot about a person who cooks for you," Susan affirms. "If there is plenty of food, then he is a generous person." Take Susan's advice: "Be sure that the meals have heart-pounding results."

Menu

Warm-Hearted Scones with Devonshire Cream

Tender Chicken Hearts to Hearts of Palm

Sweetheart Lobster Salad with Corn Nibbles

It's No Yoke: A Broken Heart Egg Salad on Black Bread

Goat Cheese Heart Beets on Seven-Grain Bread

Your favorite lemon meringue pie

Tea or Sherry

Warm-Hearted Scones with Devonshire Cream

1 cup plus 1 tablespoon flour

2 tablespoons sugar

1 tablespoon baking powder

¼ teaspoon salt

1 cup heavy cream, plus more for
    brushing

Granulated sugar, for dipping

⅓ cup honey, for serving

1 PREHEAT THE oven to 425°F. Mix together the flour, sugar, baking powder, and salt. Add in the cream, mixing only until the ingredients come together into a smooth dough.

2 GENTLY FORM the dough into a round disk (do not knead). On a lightly floured board, pat the dough out ½ inch thick. Cover and let rest for 5 minutes.

3 USING A 2¼-inch heart-shaped cookie cutter, cut out the scones. Brush the tops with cream and dip them into granulated sugar. Place on parchment-lined sheet pans. Bake until puffed and light brown, about 15 minutes.

Put a little love into your cooking when you bake these scrumptious heart-shaped scones. Serve them with traditional, thickened Devonshire cream (available in gourmet food stores) and honey to intoxicate your sweetheart.

Tender Chicken Hearts
to Hearts of Palm

½ cup diced grilled chicken breast
2 tablespoons diced canned hearts of
   palm, drained
2 tablespoons diced canned artichoke
   hearts, drained
2 tablespoons mayonnaise
1 teaspoon dried mustard

1 teaspoon chopped fresh tarragon
1 tablespoon chopped celery
Salt and freshly ground black pepper
1 slice multigrain bread
1 teaspoon chopped flat-leaf (Italian)
   parsley, for garnish

1 IN A mixing bowl, mix the chicken, hearts of palm, artichokes, may-onnaise, mustard, tarragon, and celery together. Season with salt and pep-per to taste. Set aside.

2 SPREAD THE chicken mixture on the bread, trim off the outer crust, and cut the bread crosswise to make four small triangular sandwiches. Sprinkle with chopped parsley and serve.

Sweetheart Lobster Salad
with Corn Nibbles

¼ cup diced cooked lobster meat

1 tablespoon diced seeded tomato

½ tablespoon diced red onion

½ teaspoon grated lemon zest

½ teaspoon fresh lemon juice

½ teaspoon chopped fresh chervil,
   plus 4 sprigs

3 tablespoons mayonnaise

Salt and freshly ground black pepper

1 large, thin slice sourdough bread

1 teaspoon roasted corn kernels

Taste these little snacks and you'll agree that the slight licorice flavor of chervil makes them just perfect.

1 COMBINE THE lobster, tomato, onion, lemon zest, lemon juice, chopped chervil, and mayonnaise. Season with salt and pepper to taste.

2 SPREAD THE lobster salad on top of the bread. Cut the slice crosswise to make four small open sandwiches. Sprinkle with corn kernels and garnish each piece with a sprig of chervil.

It's No Yoke: A Broken Heart Egg Salad on Black Bread

Dress up this traditional salad by making heart-shaped open sandwiches with fresh black bread.

½ cup (3 large eggs) coarsely chopped
   hard-boiled eggs
2 tablespoons mayonnaise
1 teaspoon diced red onion
2 teaspoons chopped flat-leaf (Italian)
   parsley

Salt and freshly ground black pepper
1 slice black pumpernickel bread
1 teaspoon tender celery leaves,
   julienned

1 COMBINE THE eggs, mayonnaise, onion, and 1 teaspoon parsley. Season with salt and pepper to taste.

2 USE A small cookie cutter to cut small round or heart shapes out of the slice of bread. Keeping the bread in the cutter, place a tablespoon of egg salad on top and press it down gently to mold it slightly. Slowly remove the cutter and sprinkle with some of the remaining parsley and celery leaves. Repeat for each sandwich.

Goat Cheese and Heart Beets
on Seven-Grain Bread

1 cup balsamic vinegar

½ cup mayonnaise

1 slice seven-grain bread

4 ounces goat cheese, cut into 1-ounce
   pieces

¼ cup diced roasted red beets
   (page 11)

1 teaspoon chopped fresh rosemary

Combining sweet beets and aromatic rosemary in this creamy sandwich highlights the attractive pairing of sweet and savory.

1 SIMMER THE vinegar until it is reduced to 2 tablespoons, about 10 minutes. Cool for 10 minutes and mix into the mayonnaise.

2 SPREAD THE balsamic mayonnaise onto the bread. Using a cookie cutter, cut the bread into four small round or heart-shaped pieces. With the bread still in the cutter, press one piece of goat cheese onto the bread, forming the cheese into the shape of the cutter. Slowly remove the cutter and sprinkle the cheese with beets and chopped rosemary. Repeat for each small sandwich.

Patricia Williams

New York

SINCE EXCHANGING HER ballet slippers for chef whites, former ballerina Patricia Williams has pirouetted her way to top toque at some of Manhattan's finest restaurants, including City Wine & Cigar Bar and Berkeley Bar & Grill. Patricia's culinary and theatrical talents came in handy when she invited her then-boyfriend Ron over for a romantic dinner. Setting a beautiful and dramatic stage has always been important to the retired dancer. In order to achieve dazzling effects, Patricia arranged tall candles accented with golden tassels around the fireplace and covered the table with an elegant maroon and flaxen runner. She used bright chargers as dinner plates and oversized balloon glasses for the wine. For bait she prepared poached oysters and sorrel cream, rack of lamb accompanied by a mushroom and potato napoleon, and ultimately hooked him with her lemon mille-feuille with raspberry coulis.

On their wedding day, Patricia didn't have to worry about what food to prepare. Friends from the celebrated New York City restaurants Nobu, Montrachet, Layla, and Tribeca Grill collaborated on an elaborate dinner, preparing each restaurant's signature dish in honor of the couple. François Payard baked the wedding cake and individual bags of chocolate for guests to take home. How did Patricia feel about these gifts? "It was so nice not to worry about the food for once!"

Menu

Kumamoto Oysters Poached in Sorrel Cream

Rack of Lamb with White Port Sauce

Potato and Mushroom Napoleons

Cosne Romanee Burgundy—
Nuits Saint Georges Les Charmois, 1994

Fresh Raspberries

Kumamoto Oysters Poached in Sorrel Cream

¼ cup diced leeks

1 tablespoon minced garlic

¼ cup white wine

1 cup heavy cream

¼ cup julienned sorrel

6 Kumamoto oysters, shucked (page 9), their liquid reserved, and 6 shells reserved for serving

1 teaspoon salt

Sprigs fresh chervil, for garnish

The subtle acidity of sorrel tempers a cream sauce that envelops these oysters to create a rich, complex flavor.

1 COMBINE THE leeks, garlic, and wine and cook over medium-high heat until reduced to a syrup, about 5 minutes. Add the cream and cook until the liquid is reduced by one-third. Remove from the heat and puree in a blender with the sorrel. Strain the sauce and chill until ready to use. (This may be made early in the day.)

2 JUST BEFORE serving, combine the sorrel cream, oysters, liquid from the oysters, and salt and cook until the edges of the oysters just begin to curl, about 3 minutes.

3 TO SERVE, place each oyster in a shell and spoon the warm sauce over the oysters and onto the plate. Garnish with chervil.

Rack of Lamb with White Port Sauce

For the coating

½ cup coriander seeds

¼ cup whole black peppercorns

1 tablespoon green peppercorns

2 tablespoons pink peppercorns

½ cup yellow mustard seeds

3 tablespoons black onion seeds
   (available in gourmet markets)

1 cup fine cornmeal

For the sauce

1 cup white port

1 onion, sliced

2 cups lamb stock or veal stock

1 tablespoon Dijon mustard

2 tablespoons Dijon mustard

1 teaspoon salt

Freshly ground black pepper

Two 4-bone racks of baby lamb,
   frenched by your butcher

1 FOR THE coating, grind the coriander seeds, black, green, and pink peppercorns, mustard seeds, and onion seeds in a spice grinder and combine them with the cornmeal on a flat plate.

2 TO MAKE the sauce, combine the port and onion and cook over medium-high heat until reduced to a glaze, about 10 minutes. Add the lamb stock and cook until reduced by one-third, about 10 minutes. Strain the sauce and stir in the mustard. Return the sauce to a clean pan.

3 PREHEAT THE oven to 450°F. In a very hot ovenproof skillet set over high heat, sear both sides of the lamb racks, about 2 minutes on each side. Place the skillet with the lamb into the oven and cook for 12 minutes (for medium rare). Remove the lamb from the oven and brush it with 2 tablespoons of the mustard. Roll the lamb in the spice coating and roast until browned, another 5 minutes. Let the meat rest in a warm place for 8 minutes.

4 OVER LOW heat, reheat the sauce slowly. Taste and adjust the seasoning with salt and pepper. Spoon the sauce onto warm plates. Place a Potato and Mushroom Napoleon (recipe follows) in the center of each plate. Slice the lamb racks in half (between the bones) and lay the two halves across each napoleon, intertwining the bones. Serve at once.

Potato and Mushroom Napoleons

1 large portobello mushroom

1 cup vegetable oil

2 cloves garlic, minced

2 sprigs thyme

¼ cup unsalted butter, melted

1 Yukon Gold potato

Salt and freshly ground black pepper

1 PREHEAT THE oven to 325°F. Place the mushroom, cap side up, in a baking dish that will hold it comfortably. Cover with the oil, garlic, and thyme. Tightly cover the dish with aluminum foil and bake for 40 minutes. Reduce the oven temperature to 250°F.

2 REMOVE THE mushroom, pour off the oil, and reserve it for another use. Cut the mushroom into ⅛-inch-thick slices, transfer to a plate, cover, and set aside.

3 LIGHTLY BUTTER a jelly-roll pan with melted butter and have available another tray to fit on top.

4 PEEL THE potato and rinse in cold water. Pat it dry and cut into ⅛-inch-thick slices either by hand or on a mandoline. Spread the potato slices out one by one onto the buttered baking sheet. Brush each slice with a little melted butter and sprinkle with salt and pepper. Place a sheet of parchment paper on top of the potatoes and weight them down with the second jelly-roll pan. Bake the potatoes on the center rack of the oven for 20 minutes, or until cooked but not brown. (This may be done ahead, early in the day.)

5 RAISE THE oven temperature to 400°F. Using the same parchment-lined pan, assemble the napoleons: Place a potato slice on the tray, add 2 slices of mushroom, another slice of potato, 2 more slices mushroom, and top with a potato slice. Brush with melted butter, cover, and set aside. While the lamb rests, return the napoleons to the oven and bake until hot, about 10 minutes.

Index